My Right-Hand Marriage

My Right-Hand Marriage

Corinne NoLast

iUniverse, Inc.
New York Bloomington Shanghai

My Right-Hand Marriage

iUniverse books may be ordered through booksellers or by contacting:

iUniverse
1663 Liberty Drive
Bloomington, IN 47403
www.iuniverse.com
1-800-Authors (1-800-288-4677)

ISBN: 978-0-595-49053-0

Printed in the United States of America

To my sons, T, you reminded me of who I was, and, C, you reminded me where I am going. It is an absolute honor to be your mother, thank you for choosing me!

And, to my ex-husband, by playing each and every one of my insecurities like the strings on a guitar, you only left me stronger and more capable of being the woman I was born to be, I fully accept our marriage and its purpose in my life.

Thank you to those who gave encouragement while writing this memoir and to all of my readers who now share in my story. And, thank you to my sons, my oldest who asked me to keep writing so there are 'no more secrets' and my youngest who napped until the exact day the rough draft was completed.

I stared at the windshield wipers as my labor pains increased. For the second time that evening, we were driving to a hospital in the Silicon Valley.

"Raining hard, but hang in there," Ted said, patting my knee. "We still have plenty of time."

He was wearing his glasses for mild astigmatism, making him look so dignified in a cute way, bringing out the blue in his eyes. My smile quickly turned to a grimace as a squeeze around my waist took my breath away. I let out a yelp.

"Okay, honey, it's okay," he said and accelerated our new minivan ever so slightly along the windy road.

Earlier that evening, the doctor on call, without even introducing himself, had told us that everything was taking too long and that it was critical to break my water immediately. The midwife we'd seen that afternoon, however, who worked in his colleague's office, had assured us everything was fine with the baby's vitals, and predicted that we would likely experience a very long labor and delivery. Since those same fetal vitals were perfectly fine as measured by the intake nurse upon arrival at the hospital, and we didn't want to unnecessarily introduce a possibility for infection, we had refused doctor's orders to have my water broken. The doctor had been belligerent and adamant, and remained insistent despite my request for some time to think. During that conversation, my labor pains had stopped abruptly, so I pressed the red emergency button above my bed summoning the nurse, causing the doctor to leave the room in a huff. While she was doing yet another pelvic exam, I cried hysterically about his attitude, and she had whispered, "He's a notorious asshole, always rushing women, don't listen to him, but you didn't hear me say this. Go home, rest, and he'll be gone when you come back, your labor definitely stopped, he scared the shit out of you, you're not the first he's done this to, go home, and come back in an hour, but I never said this." Heeding her advice, we had left the hospital, only to have the labor pains start up again with incredible intensity the moment I relaxed on our couch and Ted pressed play on the DVD remote.

The labor rooms were occupied when we arrived, so I was wheeled onto a cart into a storage closet until a room vacated. Ted held my hand, rubbed my hair and assured me that everything was okay, as I focused on bottles of cleaning supplies and brooms.

After laboring the entire night, my cervix remained dilated at 9.5 centimeters for over four hours, during which I had to fight a desire to push, as the nurse claimed that would only bloat my cervix and cause complications. Ted stayed with me and blew out air every time a contraction came, saying, "You can do it," and "He will come when he is ready" and "You are already such a beautiful mother" for the entire last phase of labor while I collapsed into exhaustion after every contraction.

Eventually, screaming that I couldn't do this anymore, a team of anesthesiologists, ready for their cue, were at my bedside in seconds with an epidural.

Two hours after that, Dylan was born. Ted's smile was bigger than I'd ever seen. With pride, he handed me our son.

"Look what you did, Corinne," he whispered. "Our son." We stared at our new baby for forty-five minutes, refusing to allow the staff to take him to the nursery.

Comfortably nestled in our recovery room, Ted reclined in a chair with his eyes closed and his long legs stretched out in front of him while I breastfed Dylan, wondering how women managed this without letting their arms go numb. Just then my mother-in-law, Elizabeth, rushed in without a knock on the door, firmly clutching her pocketbook.

"Ted! My God, your sister is all worried," Elizabeth said. She paused briefly to look in my direction and mumbled, "Oh, and hi Corinne." She continued urgently, "Jill calls me upset every ten minutes. You have to call her now, Ted!"

As if only then realizing she had a new grandson, she walked over to me. I'd already stopped his feed, covered my breasts and was cuddling my newborn, who was snuggled in a blanket with leaping sheep and cows—a "burrito wrap" the nurse had demonstrated for me.

Elizabeth smiled absently in our direction. Then she turned her attention back to her son, asked him if he had his cell phone, and repeated her request that he call his sister.

I blurted out, "Elizabeth! We have been a total of fifty-two hours in labor, up all night, and have a *new* baby. I think, being a mother herself, Jill would know to show a little more sensitivity and decorum. Plus we aren't allowed to use cell phones in the hospital."

Elizabeth stared at me with her jaw open.

"All I mean is this is not about her," I said. "Ted is exhausted, and you can call her on the way home from the hospital. I'd just hoped you'd want to spend the time with your new grandson, I mean, Jill will understand and be fine."

I smiled at Dylan and kissed his wrinkly forehead.

She looked perplexed, pushed up her glasses, put her pocketbook down on the edge of my bed and sighed grandly. She looked at Ted questioningly. He just shrugged his shoulders.

"Isn't he adorable?" I cooed, rubbing his warm little cheek, "I mean, I can't take my eyes off him."

Ted smiled proudly, took her elbow and led her to the bed, saying, "C'mon Mom, meet Dylan."

She walked over to me, peered into his face and said, "He doesn't have the look of a Nolast. All my other grandchildren had the look of a Nolast when they came out and this one, well, you know, he just doesn't have that look!"

My heart sank. Ted's shoulders caved in. He looked at the floor and shifted his feet.

Anger overtook me. "I can assure you he is as much a Nolast as all the others," I said, stopping myself from making a crude comment about her son's sperm.

"Oh, well, yes, dear," she said. "I didn't mean to imply anything." She ruffled my hair flat on the top. "You must be tired from it all, and I must be going now."

She air-kissed my cheek, didn't touch her grandson and hugged her son before rushing out of the room.

"That was hella weird," I said, but Ted remained silent. Then I burst into tears, Ted called for help, and the lactation consultant assured me that the hormonal release of childbirth caused imbalance for up to four weeks postpartum, and mentioned yet again that I was a natural at breastfeeding.

◆   ◆   ◆

Ted and I had met almost four years prior to Dylan's birth at a trendy sports bar in the Silicon Valley. It was a cold and drizzly Friday night before the Super Bowl at the end of January 1997. Ted's engineering degree from University of California San Luis Obispo had opened up a good career for him in start-up companies doing medical device product development, and he'd just gained a moderate sum of money from a recent IPO in the first company he worked for out of college. I was pursuing an MBA, hoping to advance beyond the menial jobs I earned despite a psychology degree from a highly respected liberal arts school, Pomona College. Our first conversation centered on his work angst, trouble with his boss and how he was searching for meaning in his career. Taken by what was such a genuine dissatisfaction with the values and lifestyle in the Silicon Valley, I enjoyed talking to Ted as it was unlike any of the usual bar-type conversations I had experienced. At first, I was confused by my relationship with Ted, lacking completely in any romantic feelings on my part I enthusiastically responded to his intense desire to spend time with me, partially for not wanting to hurt his feelings while also experiencing, for the first time in my life, a feeling of being totally understood. The lack of romance was acceptable to me, at the time, having previously dated men who may be considered 'bad boys' who knew all too well what they were doing in the bedroom. I found those relationships short-lived, troublesome and as a consequence had stopped dating men for the two years before meeting Ted. I couldn't believe how in synch our conversations were—his insights into human nature, enthusiasm for life, interest in unconventional living, positive outlook about overcoming life challenges—and I fell in love with his words, attitude and perspective on life, a phenomenon I learned too late was akin to recording oneself speaking on a tape recorder and then falling in love with the machine. Our dating period can be summed up as confusing, I felt guilty for not having romantic feelings for him, seeing that he was so smitten by me. I assumed this was my 'fault' for only being attracted to 'bad boys', and I tended to want to leave the relationship, but was never able to fully follow through. In talking to friends about the misgivings I had about the relationship, they told me to stop complaining as I had a tendency to over-analyze: Ted was quite a catch, they said, maybe not the sexiest man, but they weren't the keepers anyway—and so steady, reliable, and smart. What more could I want? Even a female boss who'd mentored me into high-tech recruiting and had coached me along various consulting contracts denied me an opportunity in Los Angeles because she believed I should stay by Ted's side and stop running away from love. She lectured me on the importance of family and children and balancing a career. I had no idea what love should feel like; I just tried to make myself feel it for Ted, feeling inadequate and guilty for not enjoying a relationship with such a great guy, blaming myself and my childhood for making it impossible for me to be a normal woman. Whenever I suggested taking a break from our relationship, Ted would get upset and beg me to give it more of a try, and I would agree, feeling awful for hurting him.

Growing up in Connecticut, the daughter of a successful college professor, my childhood was extremely difficult; my mother was a depressed alcoholic, a brilliant woman whose life was about reacting to perceived insult with unabashed rage. She complained incessantly about her lack of career options, hated being married to my father and abhorred being a mother. My childhood memories were filled with "I hate you" screamed in my face and "you ruined my life" and "I wish you were never born", the most prominently fearful time being when she chased me around the kitchen table with a cleaver accusing me of giving her a dirty look when I was readying myself for a swim meet in fifth grade. Being my mother's daughter, traumatized and hurting, I was able to hold a very special spot in myself, a place that is hard to describe, a private and pleasant place where pain is non-existent, people's projections of anger diffused and synchronicity with animals effortless. I was seen as a shy child who got good grades and got along relatively well with my classmates, but I felt misunderstood as a young girl, wondering quite often about the silly ways people formed intimate connections not knowing how to join in on gossip or cliques; a teacher even once claimed I suffered from selective mutism. I always felt like there was something wrong with me. By the time I was an adolescent, I'd begun a campaign of anger and rage towards my mother, spitting back at what she'd filled me with, and we spent years screaming at each other until I left for Pomona College attending a school as far away as geographically possible in Southern California.

Just over a year into my relationship with Ted, we planned a long weekend vacation in San Luis Obispo with a few of Ted's co-workers, an act that brought about a cold chill of disapproval from his mother because we were unable to baby-sit for his sister Jill, who'd presumed our availability when planning one of her "pampered chef" sales events.

Opening the passenger side door of his Toyota forerunner, Ted asked me if I had remembered his dog's water bowl for our long drive down Pacific Coast highway.

I nodded my head and pointed behind his seat. "Wait, though, gotta make sure your car is locked." I started off towards the Acura parked a few feet away.

Ted grabbed my elbow and forced eye contact. "It's actually *your* car," he said, looking at me with stern eyes. "It's not mine!"

I tugged my elbow out of his hold. "Actually it *is* your car," I said. "It's in your name, but I drive it." My foot got caught on the mat in a wave of clumsy movements, but I quickly regained my footing and returned to the Forerunner gracefully after confirming the Acura was locked.

As Ted slowly pulled out of the driveway, and my buckle finally fastened after many nervous attempts, I watched our cute cottage grow smaller. I'd hung baskets of geraniums outside and the watering can left by the front door along with the peeling white paint completed a rustic country look. Nine months after I'd met Ted, a co-worker and her husband vacated the cottage on their return to Europe, leaving me the chance to live practically downtown Campbell within walking distance of restaurants, a biking trail and a quaintness that was quite rare in the Silicon Valley. The expense pulled me into a tight budget again but with my car payment gone, I found the option appealing. Ted and I discussed moving in together, and initially we were both hesitant. He proposed moving into the cottage by myself, and, over time, he could gradually move in as well on a part-time basis. Uncomfortable with this suggestion, I took a firm stand, offering that if I moved in, got my furniture just right and enjoyed the cottage by myself, it would be hard to imagine eventually sharing it. Knowing myself as I did, I suggested that I sign a one-year lease, move in by myself and then see where we stood in a year's time. Living separately for a year would be a good chance to slow things down and let us settle into things. Ted panicked and quickly decided that moving in with me would be the best course of action. When we discussed it in counseling, our therapist felt as if my hesitation was yet another sign of my trouble with trust, intimacy and closeness. Ted pressed the point so urgently that I felt I had no space to think, and eventually felt quite guilty that I wasn't more excited about moving in together. I forced myself to be more positive, another goal presented in therapy, and succumbed. To help me feel more enthusiastic about our move, I bought a huge Christmas tree and trimmed it with lights and ornaments. It worked: that Christmas was quite cozy in our new cottage. And, yet, the entire time we lived together, I often wondered, with incredible guilt, what the cottage would have been like without his dirty clothes piled on the floor beside our bed, without his big screen TV taking up half of the living room and without an office desk piled up with his unanswered mail. Any requests on my part to tidy up were seen as unreasonable criticisms and he joked about the necessary learning curve about living with a man. Our therapist suggested a spreadsheet outlining household tasks and cleaning schedules, but that was left ignored on our refrigerator, to my frustration, but my friends also teased me that it was high time I learned what it is like to live with a man.

Chewing on his bottom lip and gripping the steering wheel tightly, he mumbled something inaudible and pulled out of the driveway as I buckled my seatbelt. He put Sting into the CD player, and by the time we reached the highway we started conversing comfortably again.

Within the first few months of dating, Ted had convinced me that leasing my convertible was expensive and beyond my budget. With minimal discussion, he'd paid the penalty dues for extra mileage, got me out of my lease and helped me sell my convertible to a co-worker. I drove his blue Miata convertible with a leaking roof for a few months, growing steadily uncomfortable with my rainy drives to work. His solution was to replace the Miata with a used Acura. I was lost in a whirlwind of changes, car sales, leaking sunroofs and joint car keys; everything happened quite fast, but not exactly without my input or approval or even gratitude for the extra cash each month. We had begun couple's counseling by that point, and any unhappiness or confusion I had about our car situation was seen in therapy as my inability to appreciate his generosity rather than a natural reaction to the abrupt loss of my independence.

The drive to San Luis Obispo along the Pacific Coast Highway is breathtaking, and after an animated conversation about where we'd like to live someday and what our lives would be filled with—happy children, good careers, friends and success—I eventually crawled into the backseat to take a nap.

That afternoon we enjoyed a hike up the foothills with Ted's dog and took fun pictures along the way. We went out for dinner and ice cream in quaint downtown San Luis Obispo, wandering the streets while Ted told me tales of his college years, mountain biking, majoring in engineering and his experience during Desert Storm, admitting to joining the army to get his mother's attention.

Later on in the hotel bathroom, I was brushing my teeth and Ted was already in bed, not reading as he usually did before he shut off his light.

"Feelin' alright?" I asked, climbing into bed.

He looked even more pensive than usual. I shut off the light.

"You know," he started; then he paused. "It's just I have this fear, something really scares me, and I kept thinking about it the whole time we were walking tonight in town."

"What?" I asked, snuggling up. He put his arm around me and we hugged.

"It's just you are so beautiful and I love your laugh and I am just so scared," he said with a sigh. Then he blurted out, "I am so scared that I am going to hurt you!"

I sat up abruptly, asking him what he was talking about.

He sat up too and turned on the light. His eyes were sunken and sad. "I am scared," he said, and covered his eyes. He told me about a reoccurring nightmare he had involving flashing lights and handcuffs. It seemed quite haunting. He admitted to having had a lifelong fear of police.

I wasn't sure what to do except ask, "Why?"

After a long pause and a deep breath, he took his hands down and looked at me. "My Dad used to get so angry at me," he said, "that I'd bite my lip until it bled because I was so scared of him."

I held his hand and he looked at me with big eyes.

"Look," I said. "My mother was mean, you know that, there is no secret there, the woman is a total nutcase. But we aren't destined to be like our parents, for God's sake. We are supposed to evolve!"

"Yeah, I suppose," he said, turning the light off and lying down.

I stayed sitting up. "You know, our therapist already told me about all of this."

He said, "What? She doesn't even know, I never told anyone but you!"

I told him that once, when I was at our therapist's and he was still stuck in traffic, she had explained to me that Ted's family was not as perfect as they seemed. I admitted that his mother was the first woman I'd met who made me glad that my mother was my mother instead, and she outlined a theory that suggested people were attracted to mates with the same degree of intelligence, childhood pain and emotional depth.

We sort of chuckled in a nervous way.

He stopped and sighed. "I am scared, Corinne. You are just so beautiful and I love you so much."

"I'm scared too," I admitted, "really scared. I mean, we are talking about building a life together, and we are both trying to deal with so much stuff that we need to understand about ourselves and to work through."

He agreed, and added, "You're right, though, we aren't our parents, and we can make our own way."

I sighed, "I think it is harder for some of us than others, but I know that if anyone can break the cycle of crap, it's you and me!"

I lay down on my pillow and stared at the ceiling.

He said softly, "That is what I love about you!"

"What?" I whispered.

"You are so positive, so sweet and so hopeful. That just comes out of you naturally. You are just"—he paused again—"you are just so hopeful ..."

I took a deep sigh. 'We mirror each other," I said. "So to see it in me you have to have it too."

He put his arm around me and we cuddled. As he drifted off to sleep, he whispered, "I couldn't live without you," and I believed that he did not intend to say this out loud. I let the enormity of that responsibility weigh heavy on my heart.

I pulled off his arm, got up, and sat by the window watching the moon, feeling heavy and scared. His dog put her golden head on my lap and I pet her abstractly.

I crawled into bed well after midnight, and lay awake until a message came to me: "Ten years, two kids, lots of pain and you'll be free." It startled me with clarity. I wrote it on the corner of a hotel menu and tucked it in our duffle bag. I felt it was a sure sign that Ted and I were going to be fine traveling this road together, committed as we were to breaking the cycles passed on generation to generation, and although it wouldn't be easy, we'd eventually be free from all the baggage that made us struggle with intimacy, wander in our careers and feel so insecure.

One summer afternoon, we rollerbladed from our cottage to an art and wine festival in downtown Los Gatos. Holding up a dried flower arrangement, I asked for Ted's opinion about it in our kitchen. He smiled, completely uninterested, so I put it down, laughing. As we searched for a Starbucks, we passed a stand where a man was selling silver rings with carvings. Ted picked up a silver ring with a nature scene, two trees, mountains in the background, the sun between the trees and a creek flowing below.

"The trees look like they are dancing together," I said, taking it from his outstretched hand.

He said it looked like Boulder.

Astonished, I wondered if I'd ever mentioned to him my fascination with Boulder. Bored in my office jobs, I'd do endless searches on the Internet fantasizing about living in this mountain town, imagining attending graduate school there and biking the trails along the creek. I'd never been to Boulder, except in my daydreams, but their vividness left me feeling quite intimate with that town.

He kissed me briefly, then wiped his lips, saying, "Who knows, Corinne? Maybe someday you'll get into graduate school there—they have good programs in psychology, you know—and I'll wave you off on your first day of classes as you jump onto your bike."

We looked at each other for an intense moment of unspoken understanding, and then Ted bought two identical rings, one for him and one in my size.

As he handed me my ring, my eyes watered. Fitting it on my right-hand ring finger, I couldn't believe how good it felt, admiring the dancing trees and mountain creek.

"Wanna go settle down with me in the mountains someday, Corinne?" he asked.

I nodded, with tears streaming down my face, feeling like the luckiest woman in the world to have the attention of such a generous man, who believed in supporting my continued education, a man who was ever so patient with my problems of intimacy. In an instant, a brief thought crossed my mind. As I looked at my nature ring, it occurred to me that I'd stopped pursuing my master's degree in business only a few months after dating Ted, as he'd requested spending more time together, pouting whenever I had to study, distracting me with phone calls and say that a business degree was a waste of my time. I dismissed this critical thought, chastising myself for not believing in his good intentions and concluded that he'd been right, business wasn't my true passion, psychology was, and living in Boulder, as a married woman going to graduate school, would be a dream come true.

Our engagement came a few months later, but it had none of the romance of our nature rings; it felt more of a duty than anything else. Ted bought me an incredibly expensive diamond engagement ring that felt cumbersome and awkward compared to the ring with the dancing trees.

Ringing the doorbell at my soon-to-be mother-in-law's house in Silicon Valley always gave me a stomach ache, despite the glorious flowers that adorned the patio.

When not back-stabbing and criticizing her children's partners, my soon to be mother in law was in a constant flux about the state of things: too many Asians in California, people not using cloth diapers and ruining the environment, hikers endangering birds by leaving the plastic from six-packs on the trails, neighbors leaving their garbage cans out when on vacation, and the weather, which was either too wet when it rained or too hot when sunny. They never indulged themselves in material possessions and used their money exclusively to travel and enrich themselves culturally. For the holidays, Elizabeth would give her grandchildren cheap toys or socks, believing that children should not be spoiled. In her mind, children were put into two simple categories, either good or "handfuls," with her infamous sigh. Her grown children were in a fierce scramble to convince her that their offspring should be placed in the first category while the other grandchildren should be in the latter. The competition was vicious, and whoever was not present at a family gathering was the topic of criticism as the entire group sought to win her favor.

I'd just gotten engaged about six weeks prior to visiting Elizabeth by myself. She greeted me at the door, wearing a handmade seersucker pantsuit. She wiped her hands on her apron, offered a cheek and then complained about the heat being atrocious.

We went into the kitchen, where she was making homemade jam. Spooning raspberry liquid into jars, she prattled on about her poor daughter Jill and how hard she had to work that week. Three pampered chef shows, can you imagine? All because David refused to go after a promotion at the corporate office of the retail store he managed. As a result of his inability to properly support her daughter, Elizabeth was exhausted from babysitting her grandchild. At the end she sighed, saying that nothing was left to be said.

When we were done with the jam, we walked into the back office where my soon-to-be father-in-law was working on his video hobby. When not working on call as a retired scientist at his life-long employer, he turned footage from his home movies into humorous films.

"Sit down," Elizabeth said. She patted down a cushion that likely was older than Ted, and brought me the calendar. "We must choose a date."

My stomach collapsed and I wished desperately that Ted were there, as he knew exactly how to side-step her pushiness. I nervously turned my engagement ring, a "sparkler," as Elizabeth had called it, Ted being the only one of her six children successful enough to purchase such jewelry—which, according to Elizabeth, he did only to satisfy my indulgences for material goods, because with his fine upbringing he'd never be that shallow.

As she rattled off her annual itinerary including the dates of their cruises, wedding obligations, church functions and family gatherings, she concluded that there were only three weekends to choose from for our wedding, and was I still on that kick to do this in Maui?

"Yes, we are excited about getting married on the beach," I whispered, although the night before we'd had an argument about eloping. I even offered that I would prefer a commitment ceremony rather than a full marriage, arguing that legalizing the union seemed unnecessary. Ted had gotten upset, saying that his family would be deeply hurt if we decided to elope, and if I was willing to do a commitment ceremony, why was I being so difficult and fearful of marriage? The answer to that question would play out over the next decade.

"Oh, well then, I suppose that is what will be. Maui, you say ..." Elizabeth paused dramatically and looked over her glasses at me. "*Although,*" she added in a lowered voice, "Ted's sister will be so disappointed she can't make it. You know Peter just refuses to fly."

"Can't she come alone?" I asked.

Elizabeth chuckled, as if there were just so much for me to learn about relationships, "Oh, no, dear me, Sue won't fly if Peter doesn't, of course. Now, let's see, how about this weekend?" She pointed to her calendar.

"I'll jot down the times you have free," I said, "and I'll talk to Ted and let you know." I shifted nervously in my seat and wrung my hands together.

"Oh, no, that just won't work. You see I am holding off on our annual travel plans with our church friends to go cross-country bird watching, and well, they are holding up their schedule and need to get back to other people they make plans with and, so forth, so you see, Corinne, we really need to discuss this now, so people aren't inconvenienced." Her voice had an edge that made me squirm more in my seat.

She put her calendar down, placed a hand on my knee and said, "You know, we can't let anyone change their minds."

An image of a rabbit stuck in a trap immediately came to mind. As I vividly saw it trying to escape, I shuddered.

Gathering my strength, I looked her right in the eyes and said, "I think that is what an engagement period is for, Elizabeth, to make sure people are making the right decision, and I don't think Ted and I should rush this!"

She sighed, as if having to deal with a moron. "He is quite a catch," she said. "Maybe not the most attractive man in the world, but any woman is a fool who doesn't jump at the chance to be with him, and I think you are a lucky woman."

I bit my lip to avoid crying and told Elizabeth that I loved her son very much, but I didn't think I should make the decision of when we got married without consulting Ted.

She just stared at me in disbelief. "All right, then, if you must, but let's put down May 8th on the calendar, and you can let me know if that changes, all right?"

I nodded.

We looked at each other, locked in something awkward, until I stood up and told her I had to pick up my dry cleaning before it closed. As I rushed out, I told her I would call her soon.

"Oh yes, dear," she said cheerfully, as if the last ten minutes hadn't happened. "Remember Maggie and Stan, oh yes, and Ron too, they'll be in town. Brunch is planned for 10:00 sharp."

As I started up the car I began to cry, and by the time I got home I was hysterical. When Ted asked why I was so upset, I told him the whole story, venting my anger while Ted sat in silence.

"Well, Corinne," he said when I was done, "this is how she shows that she cares. I mean, she loves you after all, and thinks of you as a daughter and is excited about our wedding. I don't think your reaction is appropriate." He stood up, towering above me as I put my head down on the couch. "You know, she is only trying to be helpful."

Dizzy and shamed, I put the date in my calendar, popped a Prozac and took a shower while Ted watched a Sharks game.

That night we walked downtown for a pizza, and I twisted my ankle on our way back. Ted insisted on finding ice at a nearby restaurant while I waited on a park bench under the streetlights. Climbing into bed, my ankle was still throbbing. I imagined a rabbit stuck in a hunter's trap and wondered how hard it would be to break free; it might lose a leg in the process.

Ted and I fought after I told him I didn't want to go to his family's brunch. At one point I yelled that the only reason we were still dating was that neither of us knew how to properly break up. When he looked hurt I paused on the edge of the bed, watching my cat lick her paws.

With my eyes stinging from all the crying I had done, I told him I just thought that things weren't going as well as they should with us. It wasn't about him or me, I said; it was about how we were together. I wasn't sure this was going to work the way we wanted it to.

As I reached for my cat's tail, she bared her teeth and bit my thumb before jumping off the bed to groom herself next to Ted's pile of dirty clothes. I flinched, checked my thumb and lay down on the bed, wondering if it was possible to crawl back to sleep and never wake up. I made a mental note to discuss that at my next psychiatrist meeting; after all, Prozac was supposed to be an *anti*depressant.

Ted plopped down on the bed next to me, propped his head on his hand, and said he totally disagreed. "That's the deal with relationships," he said. "We are supposed to have lots of stuff to work through and learn together. You teach me so much, every day, and we have a lifetime of growing and learning and living together."

His innocence moved me to tears and to guilt. I stammered, "But it shouldn't be this hard, don't you think?"

His eyes downcast, he whispered, "I wish you'd just give us a chance." My cat jumped on my feet, crawled up my leg and curled up in a ball on my stomach.

"Look, even she agrees with me," he said, rubbing his finger along her nose as she purred.

I went to the brunch. As I entered Elizabeth's house, I struggled through the smile-and-cheek routine. Gerard, Ted's father, was in the back room working on his videos, only to emerge when the food was served. Stan, Maggie's husband, was on the Lazy-Boy chair in the living room, snoring and drooling. Fred, Jill's son, was making a tower with blocks on the coffee table while his father drank a beer while watching CNN. Ted joined the men in the living room while I resigned myself to the kitchen with his sisters and mother.

"Are Ron and Melinda coming?" Jill asked while spreading jelly on a dozen slices of toast.

Her mother sighed. "Of course not. They are with *her* family this morning and refused to come to the brunch."

A look passed between the sisters. Melinda had grown up in the same neighborhood as her husband, Ted's brother Ron. They had been high school sweethearts. Whenever they drove down from Grass Valley, they had to split their time between both extended families. Melinda was the only in-law with this "problem," as Stan's mother just joined into whatever Elizabeth wanted to do and David, Peter and I were all estranged from our alcoholic families. And, lastly, Pam, John's wife, had family in the Midwest with a brother in jail. That left Melinda as the only in-law who couldn't devote the entire visit to Elizabeth.

Maggie piped in. "John and Pam want to have Thanksgiving at their house this year."

Jill groaned and her mother rolled her eyes.

"Pam always wants to have it there," Jill whined.

Feeling like I did in junior high, I sat quietly at the table, nibbling on grapes.

Suddenly, David jumped into the kitchen looking for another beer. He grabbed a toast off the plate his wife was fixing when she announced the upcoming Thanksgiving plans

David grunted. "Well, this year, will Pam at least wax her facial hair? I mean, you know that long black one growing off her chin makes me lose my appetite! It's the least she can do if we all have to go eat at her house."

Jill giggled and my mother-in-law smiled.

Maggie exclaimed "David!" while covering her smile with a napkin.

My hand went up to my chin automatically, checking the status of my facial hair. Feeling foolish, I pulled my hand down abruptly and said, "Wow, guys, wouldn't want to be the enemy in this crowd! What do you say when I'm not around?"

The silence was biting.

David came over, wrapped his arm around my shoulder and said, "Ah, don't you worry, we just think you are engaged to a loser!" He grabbed another piece of toast before leaving the room.

Jill didn't speak to me for the rest of the afternoon and Maggie was distant, avoiding my direct questions.

Driving home, Ted squeezed my knee. "See it wasn't so bad after all, huh? I heard you guys all laughing and having a blast. I even heard my mother giggling!"

"Yeah, when everyone was making fun of your brother's wife's facial hair," I curled my hair around my finger over and over, staring out the window.

"You know, my sisters act differently around you," he added.

"Oh yeah?" I stared at people's profiles as they drove by us on the freeway.

"Yeah! Jill doesn't have girlfriends to talk to and Maggie, I mean, she actually likes you, I can tell," he smiled.

"Could have fooled me," I said. I shut my eyes against the headrest, wondering what book I could lose myself in that afternoon. "I'd hate to see how she acts when she doesn't like someone."

I spent the entire afternoon under the comforter engrossed in a Danielle Steele book, only to surface at dinnertime to make a beef stew with a delicious corn bread. I took off my engagement ring to cook, and found myself making more and more elaborate meals from complicated cookbooks with each passing week.

Elizabeth booked us all flights to Maui on the same plane. Jill and her family, Maggie and her snoring husband and Ted's parents were attending the wedding, while Sue, as predicted, remained on the mainland since her husband feared flying. The group of my future in-laws were staying at a condo right next door to our hotel, their reservations made after we'd secured our room. Ted's two eldest brothers and their families were unable to attend.

"You guys don't have a lot of luggage for people about to get married," Jill commented as she hauled four suitcases and a stroller out of the minivan Ted's father insisted on driving to the airport. "Just wait until you have kids; it is all about diaper bags and toys and bottles."

Ted's parents were squabbling about how to get their bags checked in and the car parked in long-term parking. The conversation ended with Elizabeth rolling her eyes, sighing and mumbling, "Whatever you want, Gerard."

In the airplane, after finding a piece of gum in my pocket book, I settled into my seat. The horrible color contrasts on the fabric chosen by this airline immediately gave me a splitting headache.

A kid about eight years old nodded to me as I put my carry-on in the bin above our seats. "I took the window seat," he said, "do ya mind?"

"Nope." I sat in the middle seat while Ted stretched his long legs into the aisle.

The boy opened up his Lego magazine and turned the pages while Ted's mother fussed about the seating arrangements. Ted purposefully avoided her gaze.

"What island?" the kid asked me.

I told him and returned the inquiry.

"Visiting my dad in Kauai. Gotta land in Maui, then I'll charter over." He sounded like a seasoned traveler.

"You've been to Hawaii before?" I asked, although I knew he had.

"Yup, my dad moved there after my parents divorced." He looked at my ring on my finger. "Is he your husband?"

"Not yet," I smiled. "We're getting married this weekend."

"Oh." He looked at me and for a second I felt as if this boy, not even a preteen, was seeing something I could not. Once this strange moment passed he said, "Cool."

As the plane started down the runway, I heard Ted's father mumble, "All right already, Elizabeth, would you please just sit down already." I assumed he was ready to join Maggie's husband in a long nap.

"How long have your parents been divorced?" I asked the boy, mostly to distract myself from the plane's ascent.

"Since I was five." He held my hand. "It can be scary, but once you're in the air, you'll be fine."

I smiled at him and asked him how old he was. He wanted me to guess.

"Ten." I added on a few years for fun.

"Nope. Close, though. I'm eight, almost nine. My birthday is next month." He let go of my hand and flipped through his magazine while I opened up my book on animal communications, and just as I undid I undid the dog-ear marking my spot, he nudged me with his elbow. "You know, it was hard at first"—he paused and looked me right in the eyes—"them divorcing. But it got better. Don't worry about it when it happens."

My heart sank to my stomach as if the plane had dived fifty feet. I looked into his earnest face and was speechless.

"Or, maybe not," he said. "But if it does happen, it isn't as bad as you think once you get through it all."

I bit my lip and played with my earring, trying to read my book.

The boy nudged my elbow again. "Hey, what's your name anyway?"

"Corinne."

"Hey, Corinne, do you see this Star Wars kit?" He pointed to an advertisement in his magazine. "I want that one for my birthday," he said, and he rambled on and on about the Lego creations he'd made at home and what he and his friends did at Lego parties, until he tired himself out and put his head on my shoulder for a nap.

As he slept, I read the same line over and over in my book: "As we leap, we embrace the miraculous. And it is then we realize that where we are leaping to is home." As poignant as it felt, I could not make sense of it rationally. The blond hair of my fellow traveler tickled my shoulder while he napped over the Pacific. I underlined the sentence, promising myself to re-read it later.

Once the movie ended, Ted removed his headset and whispered in my ear, "Kids love you."

I smiled. It was true.

"I've never seen someone kids trust so much," he said. "You'll make a wonderful mom someday." And he kissed me gently on the lips.

Holding his hand for the descent into Maui, I let the words of divorce echo uncomfortably in my head, wondering if our children would have to fly back and forth between our houses when we divorced. It felt inevitable.

Our ceremony was simple. I'd found a dress without much effort that fit right off the rack. Neither Ted nor I were much into the drama of a wedding and we found a quaint spot on a public beach to exchange our vows. He wore khakis and a floral tie his sister Maggie had sown to match the shirt she'd made for his nephew, Jill's son. Our vows had been prepared by the minister, who made us promise to "always see the innocence in our eyes" before we became husband and wife. After pictures by the beach, the minister said, "I marry a lot of people here in Maui, many of whom I have serious doubts about. But not you two. You guys are a solid couple."

After a long dinner, complete with my mother complaining about every dish brought to her—the fish wasn't cooked well, the appetizer was cold and the vegetables overdone—we took a walk back to our hotel.

Holding hands with my new husband on a beach in Maui made me want to cry with despair. Feeling guilty, I tried to think romantic thoughts or feel beautiful, but couldn't. Back at the hotel, Ted turned on the TV while I took a shower and cried.

Looking over the travel guide in my robe, I began planning out the week, tossing a few ideas his way as he flipped the stations.

"There are boats that take tourists diving," I said, bringing the book over to the couch for him to see.

He agreed noncommittally.

"How about the aquarium sometime?" I returned to the stool by the counter.

"Jill's going with Fred tomorrow," he said, to which I had no idea how to reply.

"Oh, look, helicopter rides." I read the description, which got his attention.

"Yeah, let's do that." He tossed the remote on the coffee table.

"I don't think I can," I said, "but maybe you can get David to go before they leave. "I'd just puke and be miserable." I imagined a calm and wonderful day on the beach by myself.

"Nah, he'd never do that without Jill!" Ted grumbled, and stared at an interview between a hockey player and a woman wearing too much lipstick.

I resigned myself to reading about the Hawaiian Islands by myself.

Later, when Ted rolled over to my side of the bed and moved some strands of hair away from my face, I pulled away, saying, "I'm sorry, I just want to go to sleep."

He gasped in shock at my refusal, then offered a 'C'mon, Corinne'.

"It's been a huge day," I said, beginning to cry. "I just, I just—oh, I don't know, it all feels different now."

"Why?" His eyes were huge.

"I guess because we are married, it all feels funny." I pulled the thin hotel blanket up to my chin.

He laughed, then tickled me. "Come on, nothing is different."

We consummated our marriage, without any kissing. Afterwards, I rolled into him and put my hand around his waist. He pulled my hand off. "You're right about one thing," he said. "Everything *is* different now."

"What do *you* mean?" I sat up, alarmed.

He stayed completely calm. "You have to do what I say now. You're my wife!"

My stomach knotted up and I turned on my light. "What does that mean?"

He remained with his back to me. "You have to do what I say now," he said, and then added sarcastically, "I can't believe you fell for all of that when we were dating."

I turned off my light and lay on my back, watching the shadows across the wall as he fell asleep next to me. I replayed our dating time and wondered what he meant by falling for all of that. As he snored next to me, I tossed and turned for hours.

Around midnight, I got up, dressed and went to the beachfront outside our hotel. I sat down, listened to the waves and dug my feet into the sand. Tears rolled down my cheek slowly at first, and then I sobbed hysterically, with my head tucked under my arms folded over my knees. "What is wrong with me?" I whispered over and over and over. "Why aren't I happy? I just got married." And, with the calm that comes after an exhausting cry, I looked out on the moonlight ocean and received another message similar to the one received in San Luis Obispo: *You'll go through hell, have two children, and then everything will be fine.*

My body instantly relaxed. In that instant I knew exactly what it meant to embrace the miraculous and leap towards home. It would be a journey through pain, desperation and sorrow, miraculously awakening me to a feeling of being at home with myself. On my way back to the hotel, I kissed a palm tree, feeling temporarily soothed.

Our honeymoon was spent as one might imagine an old couple vacationing in Hawaii. We did the tourist spots, ate at good restaurants and spent Mother's Day with his family on the last night before they flew back to the Silicon Valley. Our interactions were pleasant and busy. The fear that I'd felt on our wedding night began feeling like something I'd made up. When I asked him about it months later, he laughed. "You thought I was serious?" But the chill down my spine told me that no matter how hard I tried, it was impossible to laugh off.

Back in California, our marital reception was fun and upbeat, but also bittersweet. We were moving immediately to Massachusetts for Ted's new job at a design firm in Lexington. He'd been upset about the poor leadership at the string of start-up companies he'd worked for in the Silicon Valley and was searching for that ideal spot where he'd be appreciated by upper management. As for me, I thought of the quaint and cozy feeling of New England. As a married woman now, it made sense for me to settle down near my family of origin.

As a seasoned and knowledgeable high-tech recruiter working in the field, however, I knew he had received a low-ball offer from this design firm. When I mentioned this to him, I expected him to respond with an attempt to negotiate salary. Instead he slammed his fist on the kitchen table, told me it didn't concern me, and proceeded to accept their offer. Although his insult intimidated me, it later inspired me to begin a resume-writing and career-coaching business in the hopes of gaining his respect. Within our first year living in Massachusetts, I'd gathered a strong client base, including many high-ranked professionals who touting the wisdom of my advice on negotiating salaries and acing interviews. As a newlywed, I was thrilled to be running such a successful business that grew solely through word-of-mouth networking. Vice presidents and salespeople asked me to continue our work together by coaching them in the day-to-day handling of office politics. Ted bragged to his family about my success, but complained to me about how much time it took. He didn't like people coming into the house after work, and no matter how many times I explained that that was when my clients were free to discuss job changes, he pouted and said his wife was being taken over by *Resume Right*.

By Christmas, only seven months married, I'd begun thinking of divorcing Ted. With strong professional connections and a membership in a group of business professionals who assisted in growing each other's networks, I felt my confidence in my business growing. The people in my networking group felt I was enthusiastic, upbeat and positive, and they wanted me to be the next president of our chapter, the most successful one in New England. As we drove to a mall in New Hampshire to do Christmas shopping for his family, I shared my good news with Ted, expecting him to share in my excitement. I was surprised when he unleashed his anger over my business and my involvement with that professional networking association. I was crushed and felt guilty for hurting him so much. He remarked that he'd had enough of the "cult" that was interfering with our relationship and taking up so much of my time.

We sat down for a cup of Starbucks coffee and his voice softened. "Plus," he said, "if you become president and try to run your business, you won't have time for kids."

As if on cue, I looked around and saw beautiful babies and toddlers running around, excited about holiday shopping with their parents. My heart melted. I always knew that having children was to be the most important part of my life.

Still, I told Ted that I wanted to grow the business to where I didn't have to do marketing anymore before getting pregnant.

"And you've done it," Ted said. "Look at you. Resume Right doubles its clientele every month." He sipped his coffee but kept his eyes on me.

I had no idea he'd paid enough attention to my business to know this, and that softened me further. He took my hand and told me he was impressed by what I had done. I had people coming from Rhode Island, Connecticut and New Hampshire to work with me.

I giggled. Although it wasn't exactly a falsehood, a handful of clients from other New England states was not as big a deal as he made it sound.

As I thought about what he said, a mother yanked her child back into a stroller, pleading with her to be nice as she pushed her legs into the straps. "You won't get any presents from Santa," she said, "if you behave like that."

As he got up to throw out his coffee, Ted told me I was ready to move to the next step, and that my business was solid. We held hands walking the mall among the glitter and ornaments, looking for a present for Jill's son.

For Christmas, I bought him a huge toolbox from Costco and he got me nothing, because he had to pay for our trip to California to visit his parents. To the disappointment of my business group, I declined their offer to be president, and we bought our first house in New Hampshire right after the holiday on the same weekend we conceived our son, on our first and only try, in the first weekend in February.

During my first trimester, I felt split into two selves: a woman who was keeping up the pretense of running a resume-writing business and another woman who was dreamy, distracted and spending hours walking dogs at a nearby farm, marveling at the way the sun rays danced off the melting icicles. Instead of following up on leads for new clients, I'd browse the toy stores and fondle baby clothes at the nearby mall. I'd talk to my baby boy, as it always just felt like a boy, and imagine his little feet and his smile.

Towards the end of the first trimester, my nightmares began. Fear and panic about the proximity of my mother, who still lived two hours away in Connecticut, overwhelmed me. Memories of her yelling that she wished she'd had a son instead of such a useless daughter, that she hated me and that I made her miserable, took over my thoughts and affected my concentration. Nightly, a reoccurring dream that she snuck into the hospital and kidnapped my son, convincing everyone she was his mother, woke me up in a cold sweat. My nightmares were so disturbing that they stayed with me throughout the day. I'd kept my pregnancy from her, as we weren't on speaking terms, but it inevitably spilled out through the family grapevine. My mother's wrath was evident as she berated my aunt mercilessly for knowing the news before she did claiming she had special rights and privileges as the baby's grandmother to be. Ted was understanding and willing to listen to my increasing anxiety, as it became harder to focus on my business. Eventually it warranted the concern of my therapist, who offered that maybe it would be better to move back to California, as the post-traumatic stress disorder I had suffered from in the past was clearly being triggered.

We'd put money down on a new house in New Hampshire the same weekend we'd conceived the baby, so I felt guilty and ashamed for having this fear of my mother. And yet the anxiety was becoming unbearable, so something had to be done. Luckily, Ted was able to negotiate a transfer to the California branch of the design company he worked for, and we drove across country in the middle of my second trimester, stopping quite frequently for bathroom breaks. As the miles went by, I felt ever-increasing relief to be putting distance between my mother and my growing baby.

Crossing into Wyoming, I turned off the radio and asked Ted what we'd do about *his* family now that we were returning to the Silicon Valley. I expressed concern that his mother would pressure us to do things her way, not respect our decisions as parents, and harrass us when we didn't go to as many family functions anymore once we were parents. Ted advised me to not worry. His mother and sisters loved me. The subject was closed.

A heavy burden began to weigh me down as we got closer and closer to California: I'd simply replaced the anxiety and fear of my own mother with being manipulated and controlled by his mother. As we drove through Truckee down the mountains to the Silicon Valley, my tears were unstoppable. Ted, thinking they were a cute display of hormonal imbalance, rubbed my belly as he drove.

"Oh my, you are just like me," Elizabeth gasped upon the usual hug-and-cheek greeting, "Now, Jill, you see she gained only baby, just a tiny little belly, she did, but my, well, you are certainly pregnant!" She moved aside to let us walk through the door.

In an instant I felt fat and obtrusive.

"Thanks for letting us stay here," I said, my eyes puffy from crying all morning, "with the dogs and cats and all."

She let out a huge sigh indicating that, yes, we were intruding upon her, but she expected nothing less from her children, and liked the drama of it all.

A week later we'd secured a rental in the Silicon Valley for almost the same cost as the mortgage of the house we'd offered to buy in New Hampshire. But, instead of a pool, backyard, cozy country kitchen and five bedrooms with a family room and living room, we were living in a '70s style track home, only 900 square feet with an old kitchen, tiny living space, no central heat and a postage-stamp back yard.

My mother-in-law helped unpack boxes, commenting on the many culinary gifts we'd gotten as wedding presents, sighing quite a lot, muttering that only a professional chef needed all the cookware I had, to which Ted piped in, "And quite the chef she is—it's like I'm eating in a restaurant every night." His compliment only made her frown more obviously.

I slept better in California, though, and walked every day in the good weather. I also kept a modest base of loyal clients who worked with me on the phone throughout the third trimester.

During my pleasant walks down the same path connecting Campbell to Los Gatos that I rollerbladed on during my engagement, I began to think about what love meant between a woman and a man and how limiting it was that in our language there was only one word for love. While thoughts like this entertained me and I let my mind wander aimlessly as it had in my college years, I was waking up to the realization that romantic love was not what I felt for my husband. No matter how often I tried to erase this thought or make myself feel romantic love, I couldn't, and in fact, my awareness only grew until I finally confided in a girl-friend. She explained to me that many women marry men to have children and don't love their husbands in that knock-me-over way. It was, according to her, normal and something to accept. She'd met her husband in college, and though their love had changed over time, she said, it was really comfortable and good. I would not have described my relationship with my husband as ever having been comfortable and good, but when I tried to confide in her, she didn't understand. She said that relationships took a lot of work.

Ted took pictures of my growing belly every weekend. Despite my protests that I was not comfortable with pictures, he insisted on having me stand sideways every Sunday so he could take a picture of what was to me quite an embarrassing change in my body. He loved my expanding waistline, and refused to attend to my utter and obvious dislike of being photographed in such a way.

Throughout the third trimester, he complained quite frequently about the attention that I received, saying, "Everyone asks you how *you* are. Don't they know I am in this too? I mean, it's like you get all the attention now. Even my own mother doesn't say hello to me first anymore. It is all about you." And, dare I admit, I pitied him genuinely for this. I was so caught up in his perspective and my desire for intimate connection with him that I was aghast that our society favored a woman so during a pregnancy and ignored a man. I even submitted an article to a magazine about the inequity of the pre-natal experience for men.

Once at a family gathering, after a long vent about how ignored he felt, his sister Jill finally exclaimed, "Shut up already! *My God*, Ted, she's the one having the baby, give it a break!" This ended his pity-party tirades in front of his family.

At our prenatal classes, Ted realized that he could get attention for being supportive of me, and he began asking me how to support my back with pillows as we practiced our breathing, to which the nurse gave him a thumbs-up. Of course, with no audience, he had never asked about my comfort. In fact, he had complained quite a lot about my lack of sex drive. Again, I felt guilty, so I agreed to a few activities, only to feel like the entire experience was about satisfying him, the duped husband of a miserably pregnant wife who didn't feel a bit sexy, and eventually, I just couldn't keep up the pretense. He was upset, but eventually he resigned himself to it, reassuring himself that things would go back to normal after the birth, which they never did.

After briefly exploring the idea of homebirth, I presented the idea to Ted, who said he'd think about and look it up on the internet at work in his spare time. The impending birth in a hospital was making me quite upset and I craved a more natural and nurturing setting. My doctor worked with a midwife, who talked to me at great length about the pros and cons of a homebirth in comparison to a hospital birth. The more I learned about homebirth, the more it resonated with the earthy, natural and spiritual woman inside me. My feeling of empowerment began to grow, as did my excitement about this option, until Ted's mother whispered to me during a walk at Shoreline that the only reason all six of her children lived was because she had a doctor birth them in a hospital. According to her, the notion of a homebirth was absurd, and Ted should be considered in this decision as it was his baby too and by the way, didn't I remember that Ted's father's mother had died in childbirth, leaving him an orphan as a newborn? The subject was dropped right then.

Every week we were expected to have a meal with his parents. Should any of Ted's siblings be in town, our entire social calendar was to be ready for last-minute get-togethers and phone calls telling us where to meet the group. When his sister Jill called to request help with babysitting and we refused, an elaborate and sound excuse had to be presented to avoid conflict. Simply saying "No" didn't work for us; "Sorry" was impossible. Ted and I had many fights around my growing desire for space from his family. He would say "They'll be so disappointed if you don't go," or "Jill just gave us a ton of baby clothes, we have to baby sit for her, it's a way to show our appreciation," or "It's just a few hours at my mom's house."

A few weeks before my due date, Ted's sister Maggie flew in from Grass Valley for the day, and his mother left a message on our voicemail at 8 a.m.: "Oh, hi, Ted and Corinne, it's Mom. We are meeting for brunch at 9:30. Maggie is in town, Jill will be there. Bye."

I had just poured some coffee and was feeling quite snug and comfortable reading the newspaper. I deleted her message. "Why doesn't she ever ask if we are free?" I said. "It's like she assumes we'll be there."

"That is the way she is," he said. He pet his dog under her chin as she looked up at me with contentment.

"I know, but I don't want to go to brunch. We just had dinner there last night."

He unfolded the newspaper and began flipping through the ads from Dick's Sporting Good stores.

"I need a new hockey stick," he said.

Taking this as a great chance to be a couple about to have a baby, I jumped in. "Yeah, great. Let's get you a hockey stick and then we can go shopping for some baby stuff."

He paused, considering it, and then said, "Jill gave you all you need, I thought."

"She gave clothes but we need other stuff, like cute stuff to put in the nursery."

"We don't have a ton of money, Corinne." He kept flipping through the advertisements.

I took his hand. "Oh, I know, but I don't want big stuff."

The other mothers-to-be in my prenatal swim class in Los Gatos had described their elaborate nurseries to me. Some of the women had hired interior designers to paint the walls and match the garbage cans and curtains. I was always silent during their excited chat about the themes they'd chosen and smartly deflected any questions sent my way, eventually feeling smug and self-righteous: having a baby wasn't about decorating a room, I reasoned; it was about preparing yourself for motherhood. But now, even though I still thought they were excessive, I saw their point: when you have a baby, it's fun to bring that baby into a room that's positive and beautiful.

"We need sheets for the crib," I said. "Little toys and stuff."

His eyes lit up. As a boy, he had been repeatedly dragged out of toy stores screaming in temper tantrums that embarrassed his parents. As an adult, he was happy to find that shopping could be an enjoyable experience.

"We have to do brunch," he said, "but let's go tomorrow. There's a Babies R Us down near Gilroy."

"I would really like to go today," I said. "Plus, I don't want to go to brunch." I accidentally stomped my foot down on the dog's tail, making her jump in fright, and Ted scolded me for scaring her. I bent down to pet her head and gave her a kiss on the nose.

"I just don't want to go and deal with it all," I whined. "Just go by yourself."

"You know we can't do that." He was whining now too.

"Dammit! Why?"

"My mother will think something is wrong!" His voice matched mine in anger.

"So, tell her we are fine, that I am fine," I said. "Can't you do that?"

"Don't get snippy with me!" He pounded his fist on the table. The dog retreated into our bedroom, her tail between her legs.

"Okay, okay, sorry," I said, crying now. "I just don't want to go, Ted, isn't that allowed?"

"Of course it is," he said, his tone softening too. "But Maggie is in town, and so it's different. We have to go. It'll be noticed if we don't."

He expected me to succumb at this point, but I didn't this time. "My *God*, we saw Maggie three weeks ago, and unless she's finally decided to come out of the closet, I can't see any reason to have to deal with more stories of her softball games and how wrong everything is with everyone but her!"

Ted looked at me stunned, then laughed and asked me if I really thought she was gay. I nodded. I told him that his mother would have freaked out if her perfect clan included a lesbian, which was probably why Maggie had married Stan. After he thought about it, he said it all made sense; after all, she was always hanging around gay friends.

After I cleaned up the dishes from breakfast, I told Ted I was going to take a shower, and I really didn't want to go to brunch.

He followed me into the bedroom. "Corinne, we have to go. If we don't my mother will worry."

"About WHAT?" I screamed.

"You and the baby," he said calmly.

"Well tell her to chill herself out and if there is any problem, we'll call. I don't understand why she has to *see* me. I don't want to go!" I flopped on the bed, exhausted.

He just looked at me and said, "Corinne, my mother loves you and she worries. Will you please get dressed and stop being so difficult? We'll go shopping tomorrow."

I knew I wasn't getting out of it, and would be annoyed to the point of exhaustion if I continued trying, so I just resigned myself to attending brunch. As compensation, I promised myself a relaxing nap with a good book after the brunch to make up for a morning lost in mandatory family obligations.

Just six days after Dylan was born, I tried again to make a stand, this time for Thanksgiving dinner. We were both sleep-deprived, adjusting to our newborn and dealing with my postpartum depression.

After his mother left the fifth phone message on our machine before 9:30 a.m., Ted got up to call her. After listening to her in silence for ten minutes, he hung up and then looked at me with an imploring look.

Standing in our tiny bedroom, I stomped my foot. "Oh, no, Ted, no way! I am NOT going," I said.

Dylan was sleeping on our king-sized bed after a long feed, nestled between two pillows.

"C'mon, Corinne, everyone wants to meet him," Ted begged.

"No! We already told them that we weren't going, remember?"

"Yes, but that was a month ago," Ted said.

"Huh?" I rolled my eyes. "That makes *no* sense!"

On my therapist's advice, we'd had a special dinner with Ted's parents prior to my due date, and explained that after the baby was born, we were not going to attend Thanksgiving with our new baby as it was such a big crowd. His mother had sighed the entire meal, said "Oh, oh, okay" in that guilt-inducing way, and Ted had stayed firm, despite efforts to sway us. "This year," he said, "we are having Thanksgiving just the three of us, for our first Thanksgiving."

At seven o'clock on Thanksgiving morning, we'd gotten a frantic message on our answering machine from Ted's sister Sue, who was "shocked" to learn we weren't going to be there. Maggie called an hour later to talk about it. "It isn't right," she said on our answering machine, "and it is upsetting Mom." When that call remained ignored, Jill called to say, "It is hard being new parents, I understand, but you can't upset Mom like this." Ted called back, only to be berated in tag-team for wanting a quiet and relaxing holiday meal.

"Corinne," he had said, after he hung up. "C'mon, they want to see us."

I explained to him that they were all petrified that we were being independent and couldn't handle the idea that we weren't doing his mother's bidding. "She is making your sisters call us and give guilt trips," I said. "We are staying *here*."

"You never acted like this before," Ted whined.

"I wasn't a mother before, Ted, and I don't want to breastfeed around all those know-it-alls right now. I don't want to deal with all of them and their critical bullshit. I want to be private, enjoy our little new family and to hell with them!"

"Corinne!"

"I mean every word," I said. "We already said we weren't going and they can't guilt us into it."

"You are being unreasonable!"

"Yup, sure am," I said. "And I gave birth six days ago. I am entitled! You'd think your mother would understand that, having popped out so many herself."

"You aren't being nice!" he said, cracking a smile at the same time.

"Nope, I'm not," I said. I pointed out to him that even though my sister had flown out to visit us to help out with the baby, she was respecting our space for Thanksgiving and was constantly asking how she could help us out. I was not going to his mother's house and pretend to have fun. The nurses had all advised me not to do what my family wanted, but to take care of myself, so that's what I was trying to do! He grunted.

"We gave her *a month* of notice," I said, "and she is being a drama queen!"

He pointed his finger in my face. "*You* are being a drama queen," he said. "Women give birth all the time and that doesn't justify hurting other people!"

I screamed, "I am *not* hurting them! I just want some space, and if they want to pout, it is their choice!" I picked up Dylan's diaper bag and threw it in rage at the wall.

We stared at each other, stunned. Dylan slept through it all.

Ted walked out of the room, mumbling that I was "out of control" and "crazy."

Less than nine months later, Ted had secured a job at a promising start-up company in Massachusetts, and we left the Silicon Valley. He feared that we'd end up getting divorced from living so close to his mother. I'd wanted to stay in California, find a better rental, and have all of our children first, as pregnancy was impossible for me back East because being there triggered my post-traumatic stress disorder. I suggested that we try to deal with his family rather than run away from the problem, and in a few years plan a return to New England, as I agreed that it was a wonderful place for our children to grow up. He was convinced our marriage was in jeopardy from living so close to his mother, and had always seemed panicked about having to shoo his mother away on her frequent and unannounced visits to our house. And so we moved to Wilmington, Massachusetts. Dylan was a little less than a year old, and Ted's career was looking bright as he began working at a medical device company that made insulin pumps for diabetics.

But Ted almost got fired during his first month at his new job, as the CEO didn't like his attitude and lack of motivation. Ted was responsible for flying to New Jersey to manage a consulting group doing a preliminary design. Over seventy-five percent of the time he missed his commuter flight and arrived late. He felt that having a new baby, being sleep-deprived, having recently moved into a new house and having a hormonal, postpartum wife were reasonable and convenient excuses. The CEO, unwilling to tolerate this, angrily exclaimed, "Other people have these things too, but they are still able to do their job." Two months later, to Ted's relief, the CEO was fired, and Ted's job responsibilities were diminished to accommodate his stressful life.

I had stopped accepting referrals for *Resume Right*, unable to balance my career with motherhood, a decision made a few weeks postpartum when returning from a client meeting to find Dylan crying, hungry and ignored while Ted watched a football game claiming his son was inconsolable. But, I was excited to be settling down in New England. We had a beautiful third-of-an-acre yard surrounded on three sides by wetlands. Huge trees and boulder lined the property, and frequently we'd spot turtles, squirrels, birds, snakes and raccoons. Dylan and I spent hours raking leaves, climbing rocks, planting flowers, and watching the wildlife. Our house was cozy as well: I'd taken the advice of our realtor who suggested that we open a credit card for furniture and decorating, and with the inevitable house appreciation pay the card off in a year or so, as so many of her clients maxed themselves out with a mortgage only to realize they forgot to consider furniture. In those first few months, Ted and I enjoyed trips to furniture stores and quaint New England shops filled with crafts. Living in our house brought me joy and comfort. I felt incredibly fortunate. I filled our big country kitchen with the smell of baking banana bread or lasagna.

Befriending the lawyer who'd closed on our house and who had a daughter roughly Dylan's age, I invited him and his family to brunch. His wife and I were enjoying a casual conversation about the changes motherhood brings while I made a zucchini quiche and she grated the cheese. Our children ran around the kitchen playing. I made a comment about how attracted Dylan was to loud toys that had bright lights, and she said that her daughter was the same way, but she refused to buy them. Meanwhile, the men were sitting on the couch in deep conversation, and I overheard Ted saying, "Yeah and they just don't understand about our desire for independence."

The lawyer said, "I know, family can be hard. We're lucky; ours is supportive." His father owned the law firm he was working in.

"Only about twenty minutes to cook the quiche," I said to the men. "Wanna take the kids outside for a bit? There are great leaves to play with."

Looking relieved, the lawyer jumped up and said "Sure," as Ted grudgingly stood up.

I felt a wave of embarrassment flush through me. In social situations, Ted tended to complain and solicit pity about the many struggles life posed for him. I sent a silent plea to him to lighten up and stop being such a whiner, and then went to the kitchen to enjoy a cup of tea with the lawyer's wife while the kids played.

Needless to say, that friendship did not blossom. After they left, Ted said that they would never be friends with us. To my questioning face he replied, "People like that think they are better than us."

I thought for a second. "Yeah, I suppose, they are a bit of the silver spoon types, but I think we can connect on parenting stuff and hang out once in awhile."

"I tell you Corinne, it will never fly." He shrugged his shoulders. "I mean, try if you want, but I can just tell."

I'd never experienced this. My entire adult life had been about having friends, too many friends many times to honor well, but I'd never had to "try" to make them. In fact, a co-worker at Hewlett-Packard had once commented to me as we fixed our hair in the bathroom, "You are one of those lucky ones. You just have friends. People just flock to you." When we moved to Massachusetts, I had assumed that friends would come into my life as easily as they always had.

I explained to Ted that it was about attitude and showing interest in others. Discussing so many of our life problems with people we barely knew could be off-putting. He was insulted, so I quickly retracted my lecture with an apology, but he stormed out of the room. Cleaning up the dishes from brunch, my tears rolling down my cheeks, I kissed Dylan frequently as he did a puzzle on the kitchen floor.

My phone call a week later, seeing if meeting at the playground would work in her schedule, was left unanswered—literally a first in my life, a rejection I didn't know what to do with. I jumped on Ted's coattails and began thinking of them bitterly—my introduction to the social phenomenon of "not good enough and better than."

Ted's eldest sister Sue lived in Maine and wanted us to visit her as we had when we were newlyweds, and she couldn't grasp the concept that, as new parents, we weren't as mobile, or able to drive as far, or be as spontaneous. Any explanation about the changes in our life was minimized as an over-exaggeration or being inflexible. She invited us to come up and spend an afternoon bird-watching. In my discussion with Ted, I suggested that we split the driving time with his sister, as driving up to Freeport was too far for a round trip and would interfere with Dylan's nap and bedtime schedule. Meeting halfway seemed a reasonable negotiation. Ted agreed with me, and called his sister.

Crossing the border from New Hampshire into Maine, I questioned why we were driving so far. Dylan had fallen asleep late morning in the backseat, his naptime schedule already in a flux. Ted admitted that his sister hadn't wanted to meet us half way, as she'd already inconvenienced herself driving from her home in Machias the weekend prior. He picked up a map and stared at it intently.

"What the hell do you mean?" My heart began beating extremely fast.

"She said they couldn't drive that far," he explained calmly, "and she wanted to meet in Freeport."

"And *why didn't you tell me this!?*" I yelled.

"I forgot," he said coldly.

"EXCUSE ME?" I screamed.

"Don't wake up Dylan, Corinne."

I sat in silence while anger churned inside of me. I pulled off at the next exit and began driving south. Now upset himself, Ted put his hand on the dashboard and demanded to know what I was doing. I told him we were returning home and that he should call that "inflexible bitch of a sister of yours and tell her we aren't coming," adding for emphasis that it was no wonder she had no friends. At which point Ted argued she did. I proceeded to explain that a friend was interested in having coffee and enjoying someone's company, not simply a relationship with benefactors who funded her trips to South America to make bridges or someone who listened to her prattle on about environmental disasters. I added that I couldn't imagine anyone waking up and wanting to have coffee with his sister just because she was an enjoyable person.

He folded the map and tore it. "Are you done, Corinne?"

I nodded, surprised at my righteous tantrum.

He took this as a chance to reach me. "Look," he said, "I didn't tell you because I knew you'd get mad."

I gave him a look indicating that I was no fool and had figured that out already.

He laughed, genuinely impressed by my scorn, which actually lightened the mood. "Okay, so, let's just go. We'll go to the L.L. Bean, buy some winter stuff, and have lunch with my sister, and just come home!"

I whined that we shopped enough already and didn't need anything. Ted pleaded some more until I finally agreed by turning the car around towards Maine.

After some silence, I asked him to explain why he didn't stand up to her, to which he whispered that he lacked a concrete answer. Pity overcame me: he really was in over his head in the world of women and caught between me and his family—a place no man should be. I apologized and said that I was sorry for being pigheaded and unreasonable.

"It didn't used to be like this, Corinne," Ted said. He picked up a CD cover and began open and closing it over and over.

"I know," I laughed, and reached out to hold his hand. "God, Ted, I would do whatever they wanted, don't you remember? Of course they loved me, I didn't have any voice and now I do and all hell is breaking loose!"

We drove in silence, listening to music, until we eventually pulled into the Friendly's in Freeport. After a greeting from his sister that included, "You're late," we had a polite and boring time talking about the lack of funding for environmental causes and the progressive nature of the Green Party. We went to L.L. Bean and bought scarves, hats and new boots. We told Sue that that we ate organic food exclusively, but she told us not to be fooled by that industry; it was tainted by big corporations controlling government regulations, and "organic" didn't really mean anything. Before leaving, we received "Peace" and "Be Green" bumper stickers. I wondered if she ever tired of having to be the right-est one with the last word.

We then drove home late afternoon with a sleeping son whose sleep schedule was thrown out of whack for a week.

I began a relentless campaign to try to smooth out our relations with his family, but to no avail. Any attempts to create a visitation plan—going to California annually and allocating seasonal weekend trips to Maine—were ignored, and Ted got increasingly more and more passive-aggressive as time went on. He refused to do any yard work, or even to call a gardener. My suggestions that we invite some colleagues from work over to watch football were left hanging. Looking for a therapist was useless: he didn't understand, or pretended to not understand, what was going on, showing no remorse or sadness that the strain with his family was upsetting me so. Continuing to tell them we needed space seemed the only answer. For his parents' 50th anniversary, Jill organized a party inviting all her siblings except us. We found out about it when we were accidentally copied on an email by Sue about a month before the event. Ted wanted to ignore it, but I felt it was a good chance to show them that we wanted to be in their lives peacefully but assertively, and after a three-hour discussion after Dylan's bedtime, Ted finally agreed to go to the anniversary party. Many of them gave us the silent treatment, and when I tried to introduce Dylan to his cousin Fred at the other end of the table by bringing some toys over for the children to share, Jill ignored me, her husband turned her son's chair away from us and they purposefully entered into conversation with Ron's family, leaving me stunned—"the walking dead," I called us later on to Ted as we flew back to Massachusetts.

One day after a good snowfall, we were in the yard building a snowman with Dylan. The neighborhood was alive with snow blowers, sledding children and winter energy. I began my usual conversation about our troubled relationship, trying to solicit some mindshare and solution.

"I mean, we just have so many problems." I looked down at my diamond ring. My pinkie had a big callous where the diamond was rubbing into my skin.

"You should get that re-sized," Ted said, watching me.

I agreed and then nostalgically remembered our nature rings. I looked up at his face but it was expressionless. Dylan was running around the yard in the snow.

"It's just"—I began talking without thinking first, which was my tendency—"ever since we put on these wedding rings, everything has gone sour. Your family hates me, we don't have friends, and we fight about shoveling—remember last weekend?"

"I don't want to talk about it!" he said.

During a big Nor'easter, we were watching a hockey game and drinking hot cocoa after Dylan had gone to bed. The neighbors' plows and shovels were making so much noise that it was evident that the predicted snow pile-up called for multiple shovels. I'd requested that Ted shovel during a break between periods, but he excused himself from the task, feeling that his fatigue from the recreational hockey game he'd played the night before absolved him from such labor. I persisted: if he didn't shovel before bed, I said, he'd lose many hours of work the next day, cutting into our vacation time that I'd been hoping to use for camping the next summer. In anger, he accused me of using up our vacation time by making him come home from work to help me with motherhood and migraines. I defended myself and yelled that he stressed me out and that it was all just a cover-up for being miserable in my marriage, at which point he grabbed my arm and called me a bitch. I curled up on the couch in a ball of tears, whimpering and repeating, "But I just want you to shovel during the period break' until I went upstairs in exhaustion. The next day, Ted lost over five hours of our vacation time shoveling the driveway before work.

Ted adjusted his gloves and bent down to smooth out the snowman. I was undecided about how honest he was being about understanding our marital problems. Just that past week, I'd learned he was searching on the internet weekly for job opportunities at Gore in Arizona, convincing himself that it was the next best step for his career. When I confronted him, announcing that I would never move to Arizona, he'd pouted, accused me of not being supportive and whined that he wasn't being appreciated. I'd encouraged him to consider an attitude change about his job, settle into the realization that we could, with patience and determination, make incredible amounts of money at this promising start-up making diabetic tools. He accused me of not understanding the bad leadership, and I vented about his negative attitude. Every day he complained about his job at dinner. Did he want his son growing up thinking that was the way to be a man? He glared at me and walked away. I sat on the porch watching the snow fall in clumps off the trees. Later, as Ted and Dylan were throwing snowballs at each other, I walked over, apologized to Ted for my insensitivity and told him that I missed how it felt when we wore our nature rings.

He hugged me and straightened my hat as I cried, then admitting missing those times too. Dylan stood still, watching us with a frown.

I tore off my glove and threw my ring into the snow. Ted sighed, picked it up and handed it back to me.

"I just don't like this ring," I said as I put it back on my finger, "I want our other rings, the nature ones, and getting married ruined everything, we have so many problems, it shouldn't be this way, and I don't want our son thinking this is what he should do, we are supposed to show him a better way, and the negativity, disagreements and upset about silly stuff like shoveling the driveway ..."

He interrupted, "Will you *let* that go?"

I sighed. "It's just we should have had a right-hand marriage and left our nature rings on. I can't find you anymore. You are nothing like you were when we dated."

He shrugged his shoulders, kicked some snow and said, "Neither are you."

Standing there locked in something awkward we turned our focus on our almost two-year-old son. I kissed his rosy cheeks and retreated inside to make banana bread and cookies. When they came in an hour later, Ted made a fire and I read Dylan some stories before dinner. It was cozy, and all I could do was berate myself for being so miserable about my marriage and critical of my husband. A migraine intensified as the evening wore on.

I was meeting mothers regularly at Gymboree, the libraries and even the grocery store, and had two days set aside each week for regular and fun play dates. Once, at the Bedford library, I began chatting with another mother who dabbled in writing. Our children were both spirited and enthusiastic, and I felt that were connecting on a few levels, so I invited her family to brunch.

Making my favorite zucchini quiche, her husband—a nerdy, academic type of man—joined us in the kitchen offering to help. He had been disillusioned with his co-workers, feeling as if he didn't have the career that he deserved and as he talked, I noticed that my new friend and I had another thing in common: whining husbands.

After they left, Ted exclaimed, "Not again, *please*, Corinne."

Surprised by his sentiment, I asked him why.

"He is exactly like my brother, and she is like Sue. Ewww! I mean, you can hang out with her if you want, but I don't want to." He was laughing in a condescending way.

I supposed this was when we got to feel "better-than," but I didn't want to play that game anymore. I accused him of a poor attitude and agreed that the husband was a whiner, but the kids got along, and we were parents now, so would it kill him to do some family stuff with them every once in awhile?

"Are you telling me you had fun?" he snickered as he opened up a drawer looking for a hammer and nails. I'd just purchased some new candle holders that past week.

"No, well, not exactly fun," I said, pointing to the wall where I wanted him to hang the ornaments. "They're serious and sorta down."

"Down? She is postpartum totally depressed!" Ted said, "And, he had a crush on you."

I rolled my eyes and turned away to wash the dishes while he hammered nails into the wall. Dylan drove his cars around my feet and I pretended to be a bridge while I scrubbed zucchini off my fry pan. My shoulders ached for reasons I didn't understand and I dropped the pan often trying to clean it. Dylan hugged me frequently and eventually the kitchen was clean.

A week or so later, she called inviting us to dinner, but I declined. I met with her only a few times afterwards not knowing what to do, eventually letting the friendship dwindle into a bundle of excuses I came up with for why we shouldn't let the children play together: her house was too dirty; she didn't give her child enough attention; she was depressed and unhappy in her marriage.

I had causal conversations during play dates with other mothers dissatisfied with their marriages. We discussed how relationships change after having children, and these talks always left me confused and guilty. They accepted dissatisfaction in a way that I found difficult to do myself.

One night while singing Dylan his bedtime song that I'd made up for him, including verses like, "You are important tooooo this earth, everyyyy day siiiince your birth," my desire for a divorce became clear. I'd envisioned us in two separate houses, yes small, but independent, and we were jointly raising our son, each able to spend quality time with him devoid of long conversations about our problems. The arrangement would offer us each extra time to pursue our hobbies, like hockey or swimming. In my fantasy, Ted and I finally found a cooperative way to alleviate all our needless angst over basic living, I wouldn't have to listen to him complain about his job, he could make the house a mess without my disapproval and we wouldn't have to have sex, something that I was finding boring and depressing. Over time I'd be able to return to school with my portion of the stock money, pursue a career in psychology and somehow we'd have equal income contributions, separate houses and a chance to offer our son two adoring parents without the negativity, complications and dysfunction that our relationship brought. The plan excited me, and over the next few days it solidified as the best way we could partner as parents, friends and individuals. It seemed supportive of our differences, nurturing for our son, honest about my struggle to be married to him, and with long-term plans for dual careers and equitable financial contributions. I resolved to bring it up to Ted, hoping he'd agree.

A few nights later, after Dylan's bedtime, I was folding clothes on the bed while Ted read a sports magazine. We were in our bedroom, which always made me nervous, because I hoped he wouldn't start expecting any type of physical intimacy.

"I just think we need to be open to this marriage not working," I began and tossed a pair of socks in the hamper.

He didn't answer and kept reading.

I picked up a pair of my jeans, smoothed them out and kept going. "The thing is, we just fight about too many things, and I don't want Dylan to grow up in a house where people can't negotiate together or resolve problems in a healthy way."

He shut the magazine with a snap. "We can resolve things!"

I picked up a sweatshirt but put it on the patchwork quilt on our king-sized bed without folding it. "We need to get a divorce," I said. "This isn't working!"

He threw the magazine on the dresser and slammed his fist down on his leg. "Here we go again. Can't you ever let anything go?"

I recounted the problem we'd had communicating about the last visit with his sister in Maine, outlined the lack of social success we were having as a couple, mentioned my migraines, demonstrated that his vacation time from work was wasted fighting and having long conversations about how nothing was going well and concluded that his family of origin hated us.

Ted looked at me and said nothing.

"I mean, Ted, listen," I said, softening my voice. "I talk to the other mothers, and they have problems in their marriages too. But it feels different than our problems."

"You are talking to a bunch of depressed and lonely housewives," he said. "You were never like this before, Corinne. When we lived in California, you were happy and totally different than you are now."

"Yeah, well, I don't think I was as happy as you say, but I have changed with motherhood." I picked up a pair of Dylan's socks and thought how cute his feet were.

"Yeah, you ignore me now!" He pouted.

I started to tell him that if only he helped me out once in a while, it would make things easier on me, but he interrupted me. "What? I am the most helpful man I know! What are you talking about?" He picked up the sports magazine and started flipping the pages fast.

I told him I wanted him to do more chores like shoveling without getting hostile towards me and that I wanted him to take care of the yard without complaining, and I argued that although he was generally attentive to Dylan at home, to the point of suffocating him at times, he didn't help me on the weekends, refusing to take his son to a Gymboree class on Saturday mornings that I'd signed them up for. I reminded him that instead of taking this class as a chance to spend time with Dylan, he made fun of the songs and come up with excuses to not attend. I even accused him of not being able to handle Gymboree, and yelled that it was because as a child he never fit in anywhere and told him that his own mother had told me of his infamous temper tantrums and separation anxiety. We stared at each other for a moment in tense silence.

"You're full of shit, Corinne!" He stood up, pouting and walked to the closet.

I folded a few shirts before walking so close to him that I could feel his breath on my face. "I want a divorce," I said. Our marriage is NOT going to survive."

"It's not that easy, Corinne." He began taking off his sweatshirt, as if the conversation was done. And, although I considered leaving it there, I didn't.

"Ted"—I put my hands on his shoulders—,"I don't want to be your wife anymore. I don't know how much more clearly I can say this to you! This is not about YOU, it is about US."

Our eyes locked for a few seconds, neither of us looking away. My eyes streamed tears.

He curled his lip, slammed a fist into the wall, and shouted, "You ungrateful cunt! If you ever say that again you will never see your son again!"

I pulled in a deep breath, shocked, and a whimper escaped my lips. Once I gathered myself together, I said, "What did you say?"

"You heard me!" he snarled. "You'll never see Dylan again, I'll make sure of it!"

I cried out, "He needs me Ted, you can't do that!" I sat on the floor in a pile of disbelief. "He barely stopped breastfeeding and I'm his mother...." As my voice trailed off, I began to shake hysterically.

He stared at me with cold and hate-filled eyes, snickering as I cried.

I whispered, "You don't really mean that, do you?"

He nodded and then said, "If you don't believe me, just try it, Corinne, I'll have your own mother testify against you!"

The rage—an absolute fear-filled rage that emerged within me—was utterly indescribable. I knew full well that my mother would support him. She'd been quite forthcoming in her anger over not being allowed frequent visits with her grandson, who she wanted to dress in smock overalls and shower with toys. Once, while trying to see if we could be amicable, I'd met her for lunch, but afterwards she threw a fit, screaming at me in public at the end of our meal, upset that I'd so rudely dismissed her and was "not allowing her to be a grandmother to Dylan." I'd been intimidated and embarrassed, and as a result, she ended up spending the entire afternoon at my house while Dylan napped in my arms, gossiping about everyone in the extended family. I knew she would certainly testify against me if promised time with her precious grandson.

"You wouldn't," I pleaded, grabbing onto his ankles.

"Yup, I sure would." He smiled an awful smile. "Now it is high time you stopped all this crazy divorce talk, Corinne. There will be no more of that." He pulled his sweatshirt off, and seeing his naked chest made me want to throw up.

In a pile of clothes, on the floor near his closet, was his favorite hockey jersey, an old Sharks shirt that he'd purchased around the time of our engagement. Picking up the jersey, I searched for scissors in the office down the hall. When I returned to the bedroom, he'd put the clean clothes on the dresser and lay under the covers reading a book, calmly preparing for bed as if nothing had occurred between us.

I grabbed his book out of his hands, threw it, and then began cutting his Shark's jersey to shreds. He stared at me in awe and disbelief.

"I hate you and I hate this marriage and I want a divorce!" I cried and screamed as I tore the scissors into the thick fabric.

"You'll wake up Dylan," he scolded.

"No, I won't," I said, "Now what are we going to *do*? We have a bit of a problem here! Your wife doesn't want to be married to you anymore! Wake up and let's talk about this like mature adults, Ted."

Breathing heavily, I stopped and stared at the rips in the hockey jersey.

"It's time to go to sleep," he said with no emotion. "Stop being crazy and just go to sleep. You're acting crazy."

"Yes, I am," I admitted. I put the scissors on the dresser and took the jersey to the bathroom garbage. He was reading when I came back in. I cried tears of rage, disbelief and fear. Eventually I tried to get his attention by gently touching his arm, but he stared at me with stony eyes.

"Think of your son," I cried. "He can't grow up in all of this anger and nega-tivity. He deserves a good life, and we can do it better divorced. I know it, in my heart and soul. We would be better parents divorced."

He flipped me off, said "Fuck you," picked up his book, and continued read-ing. I closed his book and whispered, "My God, Ted, you're not kidding. You aren't going to let me out of this, are you?"

He looked me right in the eyes, smiled harshly and said, "It's just not so easy, Corinne. You agreed to be my wife."

I felt so sad, and knew I'd let him down. I told him I couldn't do this any-more. "Do you really want a wife who is so unhappy?" I asked.

He closed his book, sighed and said, "Look, Corinne, we won't divorce, we don't talk of divorce and now it's about time that this conversation is done." He opened his book again. "And, if you don't mind, I want to read before going to sleep."

I stared at his blank face in absolute shock as he read page after page. I was not going to be able to get out of this marriage. Just then, I felt a hatred that would become commonplace for the next five years.

I remembered with painful clarity the year I dated Ted, and how he was seen as the stable, successful and nice guy helping his disturbed girlfriend with inti-macy problems, tendencies to over-react and depression. I was both realistic about how we'd be perceived and petrified that I'd lose my son in a court battle. After all, the hockey jersey I'd cut up served as great proof of my instability, and there would be no conceivable way to describe to others the rage that builds up when you have been trying to get out of a relationship since the day you got in it. My fantasy of an amicable divorce, co-parenting our son and cooperating in our individual lifestyles shattered. In that moment, I realized that I had to resign myself to my marriage and make the best of things. So I focused on enjoying my time with my adorable toddler. In the fall, we walked around Walden Pond and came home to make a foliage collage. We enjoyed the libraries, playgrounds and the quaintness New England offers. He learned to ice skate holding onto a crate at a pond at a nearby farm, chasing me as we laughed, both of us genuinely excited to be together. We explored beaches, museums, farms, and aquariums, and bought every new toy available at the local stores. Running up our debt gave me a perverse satisfaction, as I knew Ted's stress increased with every slide of the credit card. It was becoming increasingly difficult to keep my anger compartmen-talized, and it spilled out inappropriately at people working retail or as road rage. Our weekends were filled with tension during the day and fighting at night after

Dylan went to bed. Of course, my social life, already minimal, was becoming non-existent, as complaining about my marriage was becoming an obsession.

My only source of pleasure was motherhood. I was a perfect mother. Other mothers randomly stopped to ask me to repeat a phrase they wanted to remember when talking to their own toddler; a few jotted my words on receipts or scraps of paper. Strangers would comment on my incredible patience and playful attitude. A few of the mothers I remained friendly with through play dates would remark on my endless supply of energy, joking about their feelings of inadequacy and comparing their child's snacks, activities and toys to my healthy organic snacks, our field trips around New England, and the wooden toys Dylan and I had created in our workroom at home.

But, the pretense became too difficult to maintain. Hoping to solve my marital problems, I began pleading with Ted's mother in ridiculously lengthy emails, wondering if her approval would somehow fix my marriage. Trying to negotiate ways to include them in our lives proved to be pointless as my emails remained unanswered. Ted was nonplussed by the entire conflict, not caring about his mother's silent anger and my anguish, and so we remained the walking dead. Any conversations I attempted with Ted to revive our intimate connection or plan our future in a healthy way fell on deaf ears as he tended to zone out, leave the room, or, depending on his mood, twist the conversation to my faults and shortcomings, after which I usually screamed that I wanted a divorce—to which he'd smile sardonically, once even telling me that it turned him on to see me angry.

In the early summer when Dylan was about two and a half years old, I went to a divorce attorney, a stodgy old lawyer with a prominent office in a quaint New England town.

"I'd like to talk about how to divorce my husband," I started quietly.

He peered over his glasses, stretched his arms over his head, yawned and said, "Why?"

"I'm not happy." I felt my cheeks heat up.

"Does he hit you?" His eyes were sharp, not leaving my face.

I shook my head and he laughed. "I've seen women like you all the time," he said. "How old is your son?"

I told him and Dylan collapsed into my lap, covering his face. I wiped a tear off my cheek with one hand while rubbing Dylan's hair with the other.

"Yup, you are taking it out on your husband." His arms banged his desk with a thud, a noise that jolted Dylan back onto his seat. "It gets better once the kids are grown. Believe me, my son and his wife are having a tough time of it too with the young ones. Wait a few years, it'll get better."

As I looked at my shoes, it took me a few moments to notice that he'd already stood up and was flipping through a file on his desk. He nodded to me as a parting gesture when we made brief eye contact.

I cried the entire way to the car. Dylan held my hand gently, his little fingers laced in mine. On the way home, we stopped at our favorite ice cream shop. Licking his ice cream, his little eyes never left my face, and the guilt was unbearable, knowing that somehow I had to do something for him. I didn't know what to do, but hiding behind the façade of being a perfect mother in a miserable marriage was not what my son needed from me. A memory of my smiling mother wearing a beautiful cotton summer dress while buying spring flowers crossed my mind, quickly followed by the raging fight she'd had over dinner with my father that night, complaining that marriage to him was hell, that she hated him and their life. He accused her of being crazy, and she drank an entire bottle of wine before falling asleep in a semi-conscious state. I looked at my son, and something passed between us, unspoken but strong, that would be hard to describe accurately. The closest I can come is to say that I got the sense he was guiding me to create for him the childhood he needed, and that somehow he believed in me; despite my confusion about being Ted's wife, and despite my wounded childhood, he believed in me. So, I wiped his nose covered with chocolate ice cream and kissed his forehead. We stopped at the library before going home, played at the playground and for dinner that night, I made the family a delicious shepherd's pie.

For six weeks after visiting the divorce attorney, I continued to simmer in marital dissatisfaction, vacillating in a cycle of pretending we were a perfect family, agreeing with Ted our problems were certainly my fault, crying as a result of such shame and then raging that we needed to divorce, only to become perfect once again. I was scared by my volatility. A few times, Ted would respond to my sadness, offering me flowers, small gifts or CDs with touching music choices; and once in a Hallmark card he expressed how hurt he was that I saw him as so unworthy as a husband. The pain I felt lingered in my heart for weeks. More than anything I wished that for both of us there was a way out of these unhealthy dynamics.

Occasionally, on the way to the beach, Dylan and I would have lunch with Ted at a restaurant in his office complex in North Shore Boston. One day, while waiting for Ted by the elevator, I noticed the name of a female divorce attorney on the directory, and wondered if she were more progressive than the last one I had seen. I decided to forgo lunch and tried to leave Dylan with Ted, but he insisted on knowing where I was going. Just as the elevator door opened, I quickly pointed to the woman's name on the sign and jumped in before he could comment.

The receptionist welcomed me in as I hovered around the door. Being lunch-time, the lawyer was free, and the three of us joined together in the front office for an impromptu conversation.

"Our problems are too big and we fight all the time," I said, sinking into a chair.

The lawyer shut the front door, told me with a smile that she didn't work during lunch time, and offered me half of her sandwich.

A comfortable conversation ensued where both women shared stories of their failed marriages—the receptionist having had a mean mother-in-law, and the lawyer having moved back to her parents with a young child to gain eventual financial independence. As I cried while listening to them, the lawyer found me a box of Kleenex, and explained to me that finances and in-law relations were the biggest marriage breakers.

"So, do you love him?" the attorney asked me, taking a bite of her carrot.

"Yes, I do," I said, "but our problems are too big!"

As she looked at my face, I wished she'd let me in on her thoughts.

"You know, I see a lot of couples," she said eventually. "I've been doing this for many years now, and I just don't think you are ready to divorce. You just don't have that look in your eyes."

I tried to make that look in my eyes to no avail; and I left the office feeling some hope that my marriage might succeed in the absence of said look, but the truth I couldn't avoid was that I felt trapped and isolated, not knowing why I couldn't be like the other women I knew, discontented with their partners, tolerant of men's handicaps and satisfied in that kind of marriage.

When the elevator door opened, I saw Dylan on Ted's lap, coloring in the menu from the restaurant. Ted handed me a take-out container with a salad, and I flopped in a heap on the bench., crying hysterically into his open arms. I blabbered into his shoulder, making a mess on his shirt like a newborn. "I don't know what I am doing! I am so sorry, Ted, so sorry. Why can't I just be happy? I am ruining our family!"

He gently rubbed my back, letting me cry until I was done. We laughed that he'd have to blame the crusty stains on Dylan if he didn't stop in the restroom before going back to his office. I gathered my son for a fun afternoon at the beach climbing sand dunes, retreating into the picture of our perfect family.

I felt so conflicted between my two roles—my comfortable role as mother and the painful and miserable role of wife—that it began to take its toll on my body, as migraines and fatigue became problematic. I enrolled in a weekly martial arts class, where I found a fun and energetic group of women kicking and punching their way to better bodies, and my health improved. Was it possible that the problems in my marriage were a result of my lack of self-care? After months of receiving acclaims for my front kick by the master teacher and good times with the women in the group, Ted and I conceived another baby. Knowing immediately that I was pregnant, I wanted to troubleshoot a back-up plan in the event that my post-traumatic stress flared as it had during the first pregnancy, causing panic attacks, distraction and nightmares that might interfere with what had become a relatively stable lifestyle; Ted had settled into his job after finally heeding my advice to show up on time, apply himself more consistently, respect his boss's shortcomings and settle into his start-up company that promised a large financial gain in the form of stock options accrued gradually over time. And, Dylan enjoyed an active lifestyle, playdates and recreation classes. Without a doubt, our house was cozy and beautiful. My proposed plan, in the event we needed to accommodate my anxiety during this pregnancy, was to consider renting out our house in Massachusetts, offer up a leave of absence with Ted's employer, return briefly to the Silicon Valley on a consulting project to see through pregnancy and postpartum, and then comfortably return to our established life in Massachusetts. My therapist thought it was brilliant. Ted, on the other hand, hated it: he yelled at me, called me ridiculous, considered my plan stupid and said it would never work. When requested to provide an alternative solution, he shouted, "Abort the damn thing." Shock hit me in the back of my neck, freezing my muscles into a hard tension. Overnight, I miscarried after two months of pregnancy. I held in my tears all day until Dylan's afternoon nap, and then I collapsed onto my bed for a crying fit that lasted two hours. I imagined my baby's little fingers, soft skin and sweet smile, all lost—a loss that leaves one forever mourning.

After miscarrying, my focus shifted from building a perfect life to hide behind to getting out of what was clearly a troubled marriage. And, although I was tempted to continue hoping for our right-hand marriage and entertain long monologues about the unhealthy dynamics playing out between us (hoping that something was clicking inside of Ted's head about it all), I instead began to envision life as a single mother with a career as a child therapist or writer. Purchasing a new journal, I outlined sketches of short stories, with the hopes of submitting for publication someday. Ted noticed my distraction and our conversations about geographical angst, our favorite form of intimate connection, intensified.

Driving up to New Hampshire to buy Dylan some new clothes at the same mall where we'd purchased Christmas gifts as newlyweds, a cranky old man turned left in front of us as the light turned green angrily shaking his middle finger. I made a comment about how angry people were in Massachusetts and joked that they would get themselves in trouble doing that in Southern California. Ted suddenly became animated.

"You know," he said, "I have been thinking that this is not a good place to raise Dylan." He looked at me out of the corner of his eye before continuing. "Massachusetts is notorious for having angry people and very old-fashioned values."

I sighed. That morning, during breakfast, I'd mentioned to him that my therapist had offered a few referrals of other therapists for him to try. He had ignored my comment, and any further attempt I'd made at conversation, even on light-hearted topics, had been met with hours of silence. Jumping at the chance to connect, I discussed freely my observations of people on both coasts, contrasting their values, approaches to life and child-raising philosophies.

"But, you know, Ted, everywhere is what you make it," I concluded.

He creased his brows and gripped the wheel with white knuckles as we drove up the freeway towards the mall.

I then discussed my joy walking through the fall leaves with our son, skating on frozen ponds in the neighborhood, canoe rides in spring, summer afternoons in our big yard watching wildlife and our proximity to Boston.

Pulling into the parking lot in front of Macy's, Ted's face was stern as he shut off the ignition. Dylan had fallen asleep in his car seat, so I reclined my chair, knowing we'd give him twenty minutes to rest.

Ted offered up the benefits of California: rollerblading to Los Gatos wine and cheese festivals, young professionals with similar career motives, year-round good weather and a lack of New England crustiness.

A wave of dizziness overcame me, as was frequent in these discussions with Ted. Here he was promoting a return to California, but his reaction to my pregnancy plan had been hostile. When I mentioned how confusing this was for me, he bit his lip and made a fist with his hand, but quickly undid it.

"Corinne, people can change their minds. Don't you ever give up?"

Tension behind my temples built up and I closed my eyes against the headrest, hoping to make it through the afternoon without crying or screaming.

"You have changed so much since we moved here," Ted said. "You complain about the people all the time."

"That's because that is all you talk to me about!" I said. Whenever I try to be positive about our lives or try to make plans for our future, you ignore me, but if I bitch and whine and complain, you are all about talking! Truth be told, Ted, I am happy being a mother, I love it, and I want to be a writer or a psychologist or go back to school someday. I believe we could have a good life here, and I want more kids someday, but you are all about ruining every attempt I make at bringing our family into a new way!"

He slammed his fist onto the dashboard, yelled "Damn you, Corinne!" and I started crying. Dylan woke up and I rushed to the back seat, cuddling him in my arms before putting him in the stroller.

Entering the mall, Ted held the door open for me, I smiled at him, and we looked like a normal couple shopping for our son's clothes.

On the way home, he drove in stony silence, and when we returned to our house he watched football while I made spaghetti and salad for dinner, then complained when I didn't respond to his sexual advances at bedtime. Listening to him snore for hours, I lay in bed watching shadows across the wall, eventually getting up to make some chamomile tea and opening up my journal to yet again fill pages with words and angst, having no idea how to solve our problems.

A few days after Dylan's third birthday in November, some teenage boys skipping school and smoking cigarettes rear-ended my minivan while we were waiting at a red light on the way to visit the zoo. Crying hysterically by the time the firefighters arrived, I called Ted at the office, who said, "I tell you, Corinne, these Massachusetts drivers, they are awful, we should move out of this place." Although his boss had granted him the afternoon off to help me recover, Ted had chosen to return to work. A mom in my playdate circle came over with her son upon hearing of the accident; she'd been a school psychologist prior to her pregnancy. That afternoon, she asked me directly if my husband was being emotionally abusive, at which point I refused to talk to her, requested that she leave so I could attend to Dylan's naptime and consequently ignored her whenever I saw her at Gymboree.

My whiplash was severe, and although my chiropractor offered up relief with adjustments, he was adamantly opposed to me continuing my exercise routine in martial arts, a loss in my life that he couldn't comprehend. Ted ignored my requests to carry the laundry basket up and down the stairs, mentioning that he brought home the paycheck and, even upon explaining the my request was due to whiplash and only a temporary situation, the laundry basket remained untouched at the bottom of the stairs for ten days.

Soliciting help with the groceries on Saturday afternoon while Dylan napped was just as futile, and despite the chiropractor's recommendation that I not push the cart around if it hurt me, Ted used his busy work schedule as another excuse.

Mentioning that he could shop on the weekends, I watched him flip the stations trying to find a hockey game, avoiding eye contact. He said he wouldn't know what to buy, then got up for a snack.

Following him into the kitchen, I cried, "My God, Ted! I will make you a freakin' list, all I am asking is for you to do the groceries until I am healed. Pushing that damn cart aggravates my neck."

"I can't take time off from work anymore," he muttered, opening up a can of roasted peanuts. "You've used up all my vacation time because you're always overwhelmed."

His vacation time was a continuing source of conflict, as we couldn't find a way to save it for family vacations with what were an increasing number of days spent attending to my migraines or helping me when I felt "overwhelmed with motherhood," our euphemism for my "sadness about my marriage."

"That is a different conversation," I said. "I would *love* to figure out how to use your vacation time better, but what we are discussing now, Ted, is how we can get your lazy ass to help me with the groceries because my neck hurts pushing the cart."

He slammed the can of peanuts on the counter. "You, you!"—he pointed a finger in my face—"You want to use my vacation time differently? You are the one always begging me to stay home because things are so difficult for you!"

"Look!" I screamed. "You cannot deflect this issue anymore. I'm onto your games, and you think you can change the subject on me. You used to be able to make me forget what we are talking about, but I am onto it now, Ted, so back off! *We are talking about grocery shopping because I need your help!*"

He walked into the living room with a handful of peanuts, found a college football game and mumbled that I was never happy, unable to be satisfied and the most critical person he knew. I cleaned the kitchen with tears streaming down my face. I tried to distract myself by opening up my cookbooks to find a new recipe, but I couldn't concentrate.

Walking through the living room without even looking in Ted's direction, I went into the bathroom and closed the door. Standing in front of the mirror, I saw a homely and overweight woman with frizzy hair. I closed my eyes and remembered myself in my early twenties, with flowing locks of curly red hair, cut-off jeans showing good thighs, and a tight tank top. Opening my eyes, I saw the same homely woman staring back at me. I missed myself.

When I came out of the bathroom, Ted looked at me with a curious expression. I walked right in front of his television set and said, "My hair isn't happy anymore!"

I went upstairs to read an Elizabeth Berg book until Dylan woke up from nap. Our family went for a nature walk that afternoon, looking for bugs and birds. Ted smiled at anyone we passed while I offered them a grumpy grimace.

And, of course, even with whiplash, I continued to do the groceries each week and making elaborate dinners for the family.

A few weeks after the car accident, as I wheeled the cart into through an icy parking lot, I giggled, "Hold on, Dylan, we might go stroller-skating!"

Dylan's arms shot up in excitement and an elderly man walking besides me commented on my son's red hair and physical cuteness. Normally, I would not entertain these types of conversations with strangers, too caught up in my own sadness and turmoil; I would, at most, be able to tightly smile in their direction or, more generally, offered them a scowl.

This time, however, I craned my neck in his direction and then involuntarily flinched in pain. I rubbed the back of my neck, and when he looked at me with an interested expression, I surprised myself by saying, "Whiplash. Had a car accident a few weeks ago."

He nodded in sympathy, and told me it was no fun getting old either. He and the missus, he said, just had aches and pains all over these days. She had it in her knees real bad.

I immediately fell out of my own drama and smiled sympathetically. It had been so long since I'd had a casual conversation that I was rusty with my small talk.

He touched my elbow and smiled. "Well, now Missy, let me tell you we count our blessings every day, yah know. The kids are grown, all five of 'em healthy, and you just gotta wake up every day and say thanks for the life we had."

He spoke with the simple wisdom the elderly gain that so many of us forget to heed. I paused and began to push the cart with a bit of a wince.

"Now, that hurts you, doesn't it?" he said. "Argh, I can tell hurt on a face, I see it on the missus when she goes to stand up. Good woman, she is, not a lot of complain', but I can tell a face that is showing pain."

"Yeah," I said, feeling ridiculous for indulging in self-pity. "But it's okay," I said, "I'll be fine."

I playfully bopped Dylan on his cold little red nose.

As I began to move on, the elderly man looked at my wedding ring, "Married?" he asked, with a knowing tone.

I nodded.

I felt transparent and uncomfortable as he looked at me. Then I blurted out, "I asked him to help, but, you know, he wouldn't know what to buy, has to work long hours, he's really busy at work, it's not a big deal ..."

Looking at me with the watery eyes of a kind old man, he said, "If you don't mind me saying so, little missy, in this here old geezer's mind, that really isn't too much to ask for, you know, a man doing the groceries to help you out."

He stopped suddenly, likely noticing my eyes watering now too. Quickly he continued, "But don't pay me too much mind, or go getting all upset now.... ."

To my utter surprise, I whimpered while he rummaged his pockets for a handkerchief. "There you go, come on, you're a mother now, and you have a little one to take care of."

He smiled at me encouragingly, and took back his handkerchief. As we were getting ready to go, he still piped in with a parting wave, "In my day a man knew how to treat his lady right, and time's are a-changing."

Watching him walk slowly and cautiously over the icy cement towards his gray Honda, I knew that I'd never forget the purple mole over his right fuzzy eyebrow and the way his skin sagged around his jowls. I bit my lip so hard it started to crack in the cold November wind.

A month later, on a whim, I booked a flight to California so Dylan and I could escape the bitter New England cold. I explained to Ted, and he had no choice but to understand, as he had complained so much about Massachusetts; it stood to reason I would need to get away, so I blamed it all on geographical angst. And, insincerely, I offered that of course it was unfortunate he had no vacation time to join us.

While in California, I found a rental in downtown Campbell, and when we returned to Massachusetts, I told Ted that Dylan and I just had to move into it. I contended that he was certainly correct about the geographical angst causing our marital problems, and by the end of March, Dylan and I were on a flight to the Silicon Valley, just the two of us. Happening so fast, even to me, I felt pulled into a decision that I wasn't sure who was making. Ted was perplexed, but excited nonetheless, agreeing that a move would solve our problems and asserting that

Massachusetts was not the right place for us to live. I was dizzy and confused, operating on a level of consciousness that isn't accessible in rational decision-making, and I spent much time those last few weeks in Massachusetts wondering what in God's name I was doing eventually realizing that I had no other conceivable choice but to run away. Sounding the alarm to our marital problems was futile, trying to get a divorce impossible, and yet, staying in it all unhappy and dissatisfied had proved more upsetting with each and every day. I was seeing my marriage through my son's eyes, and was acutely aware of what he was learning from his parents about love, gender roles and relationships. I knew that every day my son saw his mother struggling with love and staying with an uncooperative and punishing husband, and every day his father denied his mother the divorce she wanted, were days that taught our son lessons that would be hard to erase. I wanted my son to know love and see a man and woman wanting to be with each other genuinely and sincerely. Instead his mother was forced into togetherness by financial dependence, fear of nasty court battles, and a stubborn attachment to gender roles-stuck in a marriage devoid of partnership, with increasing bitterness and depression. It had to stop, and it felt out of my hands, navigated by something much larger than me, and for the first time since meeting Ted, I felt as if I was no longer the captain of my ship. It was was steering itself.

While Dylan napped on the plane, I wrote in my journal: *Ted is being an absolute moron, he refuses to do anything to help me around the house, and he is in total denial that our marriage sucks. Does he really think I will keep living this way? So, Dylan and I are on our way to California, I already miss our cozy house and can't believe I am throwing it all to the wind ... what else can I do? Ted won't divorce me like a normal person and I cannot keep living in this hell. He'll find a job here in two months I bet and I know, he is pissed but not showing it, if he follow us to California, he'd better be ready to listen to me about the problems we have, but really, I have no idea what to expect, I feel like I am embarking on a three year cycle through no where land, I have no idea what I am doing, I just know something has to change, and leaving Ted feels like the best shake up because he is ignoring me and everything I am saying. We'll either return to Massachusetts in three years, married and entering our right hand marriage—finally—as a healthy couple living our potential, or we will be divorced, that is my feeling, we only have three years for one of two outcomes, all of this is now out of my hands, and this is a leap of faith if I've ever seen one, but what I do know is that things cannot stay the way they are now, the way Ted wants them, me unhappy, pretending we are fine, and upset all the time, this is MY life too ... and Dylan's and he deserves something better from his parents!*

Reaching over to hold Dylan's hand as he slept, I remembered kissing that palm tree on my wedding night, along with the quote from *Animal Communications*: *As we leap, we embrace the miraculous. And it is then we realize that where we are leaping to is home.* I closed my eyes, knowing that leaping into whatever I was going into wasn't nearly as scary as staying stuck, and that somehow I would find home.

Immediately upon my arrival in California, the challenges of single parenting were evident. Dylan was acting out his confusion in sadness and tantrums, and his sleep was affected as well, requiring my assistance nightly. As I hugged my resting son, I spent hours thinking about my new situation: our house proved cold and damp, and its location on a busy street made me feel exposed and acutely aware of how comforting a male presence could be.

Drinking my coffee each morning and watching dump trucks and cars rush by while strangers passed our living room window, I remembered the quaint and cozy feeling of waking up in Massachusetts, watching squirrels play on the bird feeder, listening to owls and enjoying the seasonal cycles of falling snow, changing leaves and emerging flowers. The guilt and confusion tore at my heart and in my sleep-deprived state I called Ted late one night and pleaded with him that we plan our return to Massachusetts; the landlord would likely only charge a small amount to get out of our lease. I admitted that this had been the wrong move, thought instead that he and I should get therapy in Massachusetts, solve our marital problems with a third party's assistance and settle back into our cozy lifestyle. He refused. What was done was done, he said. He talked about having more children, and pointed out that we needed to move out of New England anyway in order to grow our family. There was no turning back, he said. He visited us every other weekend, acting like he had to manage a wayward wife whose whimsical behavior offered unique challenges that only he could solve.

Within three weeks, Dylan and I settled in well to our new lives, and began a routine that included daily bike rides to Los Gatos and organizing a toddler's marching band for the city of Campbell, where little kids brought their toy instruments and marched around the city green on Friday afternoons. I lost two dress sizes without any effort. My old friends from my single years had moved on with their lives, and so obviously distrusted that everything was as fine as I said that it was more comfortable to socialize with my new friends instead. We quickly found a handful of friends to exchange babysitting time with and go on trips with to San Francisco and the Monterey Aquarium. Aside from my house feeling so cold and exposed, our lives became more comfortable, and exactly two months after Dylan and I had flown there, Ted secured a job at a start-up company as a program manager making over $110K.

Ted's fanfare arrival—the returning hero who had made it—created a celebratory mood in our family. For the first week, he was talkative, telling me how much he missed me, enthusiastic, believing this was our first step into our right hand marriage, and attentive to Dylan, bringing him to playgrounds without any pleading on my part.

His first week of work, the Thursday evening before moving trucks were to bring our belongings the following weekend, we were snuggling together watching television, enjoying the illusion that moving to California had solved all our marital problems, when I welcomed Ted's sexual advances.

I giggled afterwards. "I think we just made a baby." I touched my belly. "I just have this feeling."

"Yeah, me too," he said as he zipped up his jeans, paused then added sternly, "Now you can't go running away from me like that again, Corinne!" He turned away from me abruptly before going to the kitchen to get a snack.

Immediately I felt nauseous and ran to the bathroom. I tried to vomit, but nothing came out. I sat on the fluffy green rug feeling dizzy for a long time.

"Morning sickness so soon?" he remarked later on while brushing his teeth.

I didn't reply, but looked into the mirror and was appalled at the expression on the woman looking back at me.

As I watched Ted's retreat from the bathroom into the bedroom, a thought occurred to me: making love to him had felt like glorified masturbation. We didn't kiss. We didn't touch each other sensually. Ever since our wedding night, it had been a cold and mechanical experience. I shivered uncontrollably and drew myself a warm bath, hoping to relax before bed. In the tub, I touched my belly and cried, knowing another baby was coming to me in less than a year.

Pregnancy was a conflict of emotions: on the one hand, depression, nausea, anxiety, exhaustion, nightly insomnia, and confusion; on the other, a new, invigorating spiritual experience was awakening. I'd have reoccurring dreams of indigenous tribes, people who felt like friends to me, and I'd wake up feeling unable to shake off that world. Throughout the day, strangers would stop me at the grocery store or on my daily walks, pouring gentle words on me, telling me I was beautiful and wishing me an easy delivery, easing me back into a life of friendly comfort lost from my single years. And my relationship with my children began to grow independent of Ted. I began to feel separate from him in attitude, thought and perspective. A growing sense of who I was and who he was began to emerge, and when he came home from work to complain about his day, I was unable to make eye contact with him. For weeks on end I was downcast around him, only to enliven at the playgrounds and parks around other mothers. Dylan was ecstatic about his brother, putting his ear on my stomach and saying he was listening to the baby telling him things, showing a new toy to his brother by placing it on my large lap, or pausing the television set to explain that Steve Irwin was going to be okay even though the snake looked scary. The darker side of my pregnancy began to overcome me: insomnia left me with only three hours of sleep per night; my anxiety distorted my perspective, and nausea affected my appetite. And Ted's boss was disappointed in his performance, refusing his usual excuses (offering up extra funds pulled from the marketing budget to pay for a nanny instead of giving him pity when Ted complained about my difficult pregnancy) and eventually threatening to find a replacement unless there was improvement.

One day, while taking our daily walk after a picnic lunch at Shoreline Bird Park, Dylan stuck a flower he'd picked into a mud pile.

"Look, Mama," he said, "that flower is growing out of the mud."

As tears formed in my eyes, I said, "Just like your brother—he is a flower growing in all this muck."

After that, I silently asked for the courage to open my mind to a new and emerging thought process, and was immediately engulfed in a true and authentic sense that the universe was in the process of providing for me and my children in ways I could not begin to understand.

Dylan, staring at the flower, said, "Mama, I melted your heart but my brother is going to help you think better." Then quickly and lightly hopping on his bike, he called out, "Waddle faster, Mama, c'mon, catch up!"

By the beginning of my third trimester, our lives were in shambles. I snapped impatiently at retail workers. Ted's boss threatened to dismiss him. Moving boxes remained unpacked in our garage. Even our dog was acting out by peeing on the carpet. Ted frantically sent his résumé to an old boss in Colorado Springs, where he'd interned in college, and also peppered it around the Denver metro area. And, although I wanted to join in his fantasy about moving to Colorado, instead I began a campaign to stay in California through postpartum. We'd gone through two midwives, challenged by my difficult pregnancy, and had finally found an earthy woman who mixed a spiritual perspective with a grounded medical presence, and she adamantly recommended that we find another home for our birth, as the esoteric negativity in ours would interfere with it. To my utter excitement, I found a cozy, modern and convenient home in Los Gatos, two months before my due date, and only one month before our lease expired. Ted refused to move into what he agreed was a good house, feeling as if the landlord was a "jerk" who only cared about making money, and my pleas that we move beyond the personal and consider the benefit of settling down for a homebirth and postpartum fell on deaf ears. Ted interviewed at a few start-ups around Denver and received an offer on the spot from a company where he had interned in college. They were struggling to keep market share and ecstatically welcomed Ted's creative problem-solving and phenomenal engineering talents.

Reading a tour guide of Colorado after Dylan's bedtime, I shut the television off with a snap of the remote, shifted my large body to face Ted on the other end of the couch, and announced that I didn't want to move.

Ted sighed, rolled his eyes and told me it was a great work opportunity for him. He spoke as if I were a silly child, then abruptly changed to a whine: "You know how it is now, this is really stressful for me and this job is not what they said it would be in the interview."

I crossed my arms over my big stomach and told him he should just try harder; he wasn't giving it his best effort. And since I was just getting into the third trimester, we couldn't move to another state.

"*What?*" he said. "Try harder? You are up all night wanting me to rub your hair or give you a back rub or something like that, crying your eyes out every night. I'm getting no sleep."

My stomach squeezed tightly, and I felt the baby move.

"I already told them I'd start work in a few weeks," Ted said, picking up the remote and aiming it at the television.

I reached over, grabbed it out of his hands, placed it firmly on the coffee table and settled back into my pillows. I told him that even though he had practically agreed on the spot, he hadn't given his current company notice yet. He just stared at me with a blank look.

I stared back. "Don't play dumb with me, Ted."

He stood up, pouted and began his usual tirade about my critical nature, inability to appreciate him and my unreasonable approach to life. As he vented, I felt his words bouncing around me instead of going into me. For the first time, it felt as if this had nothing to do with me, so I didn't bother to defend myself.

I collected my thoughts, remembered my miscarriage and his post-coital comment, and thought of how Dylan's experience in California had changed so much since his father arrived. Initially a time of budding friendships, marching bands and bike rides had now turned to long hours at home, doing errands and being quite friendless and isolated. I blurted out, "I don't want to move somewhere I've never been, and this book talks about Colorado Springs like it is an armpit of conservative people, and I don't want to go!" I stomped my foot down like a two year-old.

Ted told me I was being ridiculous and said we were going; it was already decided. "The moving truck is already scheduled!" he said.

"We can cancel it," I said. "My *God*, don't you *ever* care about what I want and what I think is the way to live our lives? You are always about running away. You aren't doing well at this office here so you want to go hide at this loser company!" I was yelling now. "I want you to get your shit together, Ted, do well at your job, move to that cute house in Los Gatos, deal with what you think is a greedy landlord, have the baby here in California and finally start acting like a MAN!"

I glared at him.

Pursing his lips together so hard they turned white, he said, "Corinne, you will not speak to me like that!"

I laughed bitterly. "I will speak to you however I want and *you* will *not* drag my pregnant ass to Colorado Springs!"

His arms crossed, and mine on my large hips, we glared at each other combatively.

Suddenly I burst out crying, as I worried about my baby's prenatal experience and the physiological effects of the blood rushing around my body in panic and of my insomnia. Ted got me tissues in the bathroom, sat down on the couch and looked sheepish. He told me I was right, and that he should have listened to me when I had proposed my pregnancy plan in Massachusetts.

I was momentarily shocked by his admission, but I quickly replaced that with righteous indignation. I put my face in his and yelled, "You should listen to me *now*! Let's stay here, have the baby and not move. Will you *please* stop messing everything up for us?"

Pushing me back, he waved his finger in my face and said, "Shut up, you bitch!"

I sat on the floor and cried shamelessly while he watched me with a blank face. Eventually wiping my nose on my sleeve, I said, "Ted, all I am saying is that I don't want to move to Colorado Springs. I think that will mess things up for us more, and I love my midwife now ..."

"Yeah, after you went through two others," he said sarcastically.

Reflecting on whether that fact was a fault of mine, a result of my neediness or an obvious sign of my difficult nature, I eventually decided that it didn't matter; somehow each midwife had added in her own special way to the care of my growing baby, and the strength of a new thought process was growing inside me along with my baby.

I looked at my feet and a tear rolled down my cheek. I told Ted that our problems were too big. We needed help, and we needed to do that for our children. "We should be divorced, for God's sake, not living like this!"

"You're crazy! Talking about right hand marriage one minute and divorce the next. What do you *want*, Corinne?" He was irate.

"I want a divorce!" I cried. "I have wanted one for a long time, but now we have another son." I wiped tears roughly off my cheeks, "It is so confusing, I want him so much, I love him so much, but this isn't how it should be! I feel so trapped."

He stood with a stony face that was impossible to interpret.

"And, anyway, I just think moving to Colorado Springs will make everything worse, and I am scared," I whimpered in an attempt to settle down.

"Corinne," he said, his voice completely softened, "our marriage has never had the chance it deserves. We've lived on the East Coast where you can't be pregnant being close to your mother, and we always fight in California living in my mother's backyard. So let's go to Colorado and give our family and our marriage the chance we've never had."

He seemed so sincere and hopeful. And I felt exhausted and utterly jerked around.

I whispered, "I'd move to the moon if it meant our marriage might have a chance." And I meant every word, knowing that our marriage was in bigger trouble than even I could figure out.

Flying to Colorado during the eighth month of pregnancy, I almost passed out from the altitude sickness upon disembarking the airplane. Dizzy and disoriented, I fell into a bench and put my head between my legs, feeling a rush of blood go to my baby. I was only beginning to understand the primal and powerful desire a mother has to protect her children. My last weeks of pregnancy were spent secluded in a small town called Monument, about twenty minutes north of Colorado Springs. Ted enjoyed the prestige he received at work, feeling like he was finally being recognized properly—"a king among peons," I'd call him with a laugh. Aside from my midwife, the only contact I had with anyone was with an electrician who had set up our alarm system one afternoon, telling me about his call to the area to do God's work and wasn't I blessed to be there too. I cried hysterically every night before bed and didn't talk to Ted, except to make sarcastic comments.

My water broke Easter morning at eight o'clock as I was rolling my almost-ten-month pregnant body over to get out of bed. We were on the eve of a hospital-induced birth when to my relief labor began quickly. Ted immediately called the midwife as I served Dylan breakfast.

Rummaging around the laboring pool again looking for the thermometer to check it for the third time in fifteen minutes, Ted was restless. Dylan was downstairs watching the midwife boil her toils. I felt a phenomenal squeeze around my lower abdomen, and it took my entire concentration to focus on breathing. I stared intently on the wooden knob of my dresser until the contraction was done.

In a clenched voice, I told Ted the temperature was fine; the midwife had just checked it before going downstairs. Just as another labor pain began, I managed to plead with him to look me in the eyes or hold my hand or something and be with me when the squeeze came; it really helped. Ted's blue eyes, concerned, locked onto mine as I rode through the pain of another contraction.

"Colin's coming today Mama!" Dylan had gleefully exclaimed over breakfast as I clutched the table bent over at what was the beginning of intense labor. Across the field behind our back yard, people dressed in their best spring clothes walked through the church parking lot to Easter services. Grabbing a piece of banana bread off the tray, Dylan announced, "I am saving him this piece to eat."

As another labor pain intensified, I watched him butter the bread and place it on a napkin for his little brother. I hugged him once the squeeze subsided, knowing his life was going to change dramatically. As I felt his soft red hair tickle my neck, I had an uncomfortably strong premonition that, in some unknown way, mine was also going to be forever affected.

"I need to push now, dammit!" I crawled out of the birthing tub towards my bed just in time to keel over into a bent position from what was an incredible pain.

Upon confirming that my cervix was dilated to a full ten centimeters, my midwife helped me onto the bed, suggesting that I lie on the left side, as that was how she'd pushed out eight of her ten children. Her concerned and loving eyes rested on my naked body as she helped me adjust to a comfortable position for the final phase. Ted had found Diane for me before we left California as my anger about moving prevented me from attending to matters like that. My first prenatal appointment was spent bonding with her about our childhood experiences with abusive alcoholic mothers. I trusted her immediately.

"Push, Corinne, that's my girl, c'mon now," Diane was holding my leg up towards the ceiling, and I screamed in pain.

"He's coming, honey," Ted said. "I can see his hair." Then he and Diane simultaneously yelled "*Shit! Push!*"

What they had seen was Colin's blue head, at just the moment when I sighed in exhaustion after my push. A seasoned midwife who immediately sensed my hesitation, Diane screamed, "If you want your baby alive, you'd better damn well push now, Corinne!"

Her command snapped me into some primal place and made me push down harder than I'd ever imagined possible, causing little feet to kick me on their way out, a congratulatory gasp from Diane, and a relieved Oh-thank-God from Ted.

A wilderness birth, she'd called it, as she drew me a bath after checking Colin's vitals. He was a perfectly healthy eleven-pound, two-ounce baby. As she complimented me on what was, in her mind, an amazing birth—and so quick too, only three hours from start to finish—I eased into a steamy bubble bath. Dylan threw his Rescue Heroes into the birthing tub in the bedroom while Ted held his newest son on the rocking chair. Slowly, Diane began outlining all the postpartum safety procedures and I listened intently, although my thoughts wandered frequently towards Colin and his birth. A new and growing sense of pride was blossoming within me, a powerful and unusual feeling.

With Dylan in bed, the television downstairs, and Diane's adamant instructions that I not walk the stairs for at least three days, Ted and I were forced into conversation. I had called my sister, whom I'd lost touch with over the years, to announce Colin's birth, while he hadn't called anyone in his family. When I recommended he call his mother, he refused, but a week later, upon hearing the news through the grapevine, Elizabeth eagerly believed Ted's excuse that he had been too busy taking care of his needy wife to call. She wrote him a long email expressing her concern that he not only had such an important career, but also had to work so hard to take care of his wife, who required so much attention, and a newborn.

Just as I was wondering what to say to Ted, Colin turned around and began gnawing on his father's fingers, so I lifted him up for a feed without interrupting his sleep.

I told Ted that I wanted to talk together about how we would raise two children. Their age differences were pretty big, and I was concerned that Dylan would be bored staying home so much. He was used to being so active, and I didn't know anyone in Monument … I was already feeling overwhelmed by our situation.

"You can handle it, Corinne," he said, kissing Colin's foot.

"I know I can, I mean, women do this all the time," I said. "It's just that I want us to figure out how to do this together." I paused, trying to figure out what I wanted to ask for, then added, "You know, like a plan for Dylan. We should figure out how to have him get know some of the kids here. Don't you know some people at work who have kids? You could do stuff on the weekends …"

He was silent and shrugged his shoulders. We'd agreed to homeschool, initially because Dylan was advanced in so many academic areas, and continued by default as the multiple moves challenged any community connections, but I was gaining a growing concern for what was an unhealthy and isolated lifestyle for a preschooler.

As he rose from the bed and took off his sweatshirt, I suggested that we find a little play program for Dylan in the mornings, preschool even, and Ted could drive him there on the way to work. It would be a hard transition for Dylan—he'd spent so much time with me—but they could take it as a chance to bond. "You could really be there," I said, "to help him get out there and make new friends."

He stared at me in disbelief.

As a child, Ted had cried and thrown tantrums when dropped off for school. I thought this might be a chance for him to empathize with his son and create a special connection; but he refused.

"I am surprised to hear that come out of your mouth," he said. "School? You never wanted to do that!" He spoke in a mocking tone.

With tears in my eyes I explained that I never thought school was bad; I just thought we should be choosey instead of just enrolling in a local school just because. I just thought that Ted could be a really big part of Dylan's life and could lead him into this new experience and that would be good for him.

He stared coldly at me and reluctantly walked over to sit on the bedside.

"Can't you just join a mother's group or something?" he asked, seeming like he'd rather be doing anything else than talking to me about such a banal subject.

I covered my head in my hands and cried shamelessly until I eventually calmed down and told Ted that I needed us to partner about this. "Maybe you can come up with ideas to do with Dylan on the weekends," I said, "or help him with the preschool thing. I just think you should be more involved in your son's life!"

I immediately stopped, frozen. He was glaring at me. "Involved? Are you saying that I am not involved in my son's life?"

I actually started to stutter as my heart raced. I told Ted I just wanted him to help me, not by cleaning the house this time, and not by shopping, but by being a good father for our son. "Stop acting like everything is about *you*," I said. "He needs a role model, a guide and a father."

He stood up, put his face so close that his nose rubbed mine and said, "I am his father, you bitch!" He proceeded to complain about my lack of appreciation for him, my critical nature and my inability to be satisfied, concluding by saying that I wouldn't know a good husband if I were married to one.

I said sarcastically and loudly, "Ted, a good man listens to what his wife is saying instead of trying to convince her he is something he isn't!"

He leaned over our peacefully sleeping newborn and yelled, "Fuck you, you fucking cunt!" so loudly that Colin rolled over and leaned into me.

In what felt like slow motion, I picked up my baby, just eight hours old, and put him to my breast. I hissed to my husband to get the hell out of my life. He stood unmoving, watching me cry as I fed our newborn.

"You are a beautiful mother," he offered me by way of apology.

"You need to go," I said. "You cannot stay here tonight." I surprised myself with my authority.

"Where should I go?" he asked downheartedly.

"I don't know, a hotel or something. Maybe where they put us up when we first got here." I placed Colin back down on the bed beside me.

"Look, Corinne, I shouldn't have said that." Ted took a step closer to the bed.

"No, you shouldn't have, Ted, and the real deal here now is not even that I am mad, it is that I need to sleep, and I won't be able to rest with you here." I was calm and logical.

"Well, it's not like you were behaving perfectly yourself, Corinne. Don't act so high and mighty."

"Ted, I am done with this tonight. You have to go to a hotel." I turned off the light next to my bed and settled down as if I was going to sleep. When he remained there, I said, "For God's sake, Ted, I gave *birth* this morning, just go already and give me some freaking space!"

Slamming the front door on his way out, Ted woke up Dylan, who then crawled into bed with me. With my two young and needy sons nestled beside me in a king-sized bed, I cried silent tears so as to not disturb them. I felt completely overwhelmed.

Growing hungry, I realized that Diane had forbidden me to go downstairs, which made me cry even more helplessly. For over an hour I sat on the bathroom floor, hungry, sobbing, and wiping my eyes roughly with toilet paper.

The next day we agreed that stress had made us both say things we regretted, but in my mind something had forever changed—an irreversible shift. Colin's birthday, his first night in the world, was the first night I forced his father to sleep in a hotel. I felt a lonely strength and powerful conviction beginning to emerge.

Ted's company gave him two weeks of paid time off postpartum, and I recovered quickly from my homebirth. Dylan was showing increasing signs of anger towards Ted, although his adjustment to being a big brother was fluid: he'd place toys on the floor next to his brother sleeping in the bassinet, and jump in excitement when it was time to have "wake-up time with the baby." Realizing that Monument was not a hotbed of activities and that we were homebound in a remote town with a colicky baby who screamed whenever we drove in the car, I decided to embark on a dinosaur-learning project with Dylan. I ordered dinosaur books, puzzles, activity books and fossil kits with the hope that they would entertain him during the postpartum period.

Aside from a weekly trek to the grocery store in Colorado Springs, with Colin upset after fifteen minutes, we stayed close to home. Occasionally, we'd take walks in a nearby park lined with trees, or Dylan biked as I walked behind on a trail along the Air Force Base. But our days were slow and long and very lonely.

On the weekends, we drove to Boulder and spent the weekends in that oasis of progressive people who lived by a mountain creek. I was drawn to Boulder on an energetic level, appreciating its quaintness and community of athletic and earthy people, a town where organic food was a must, attachment parenting required and a wardrobe of yoga pants and fleece necessary. Every weekend we spent there made me feel as if I'd found my niche.

To pass the time back in Monument, my idea for dinosaur learning provided fun and distraction for both Dylan and me during what were long summer months with my beautiful and cuddly newborn.

Bedtime was the hardest time for us as a family: Dylan would get visibly angry at his father, punching him and refusing to sit quietly for book time. Ted acted insulted and hurt by his son's behavior, and at times used force that made me uncomfortable.

"No! Tee, no!" Dylan yelled at his father, whom he'd called Dad only briefly, but had quickly replaced with "Tee" by the time he was eighteen months. I was calming Colin into his bedtime feed and overheard more screams. "I said NO, Tee!"

My requests that they settle down were ignored and I heard Ted's stern and angry voice yell his son's full name, causing me to shiver. Hearing the *Dylan Nolast* from his voice, I rushed to the bathroom with Colin latched on to one breast.

Walking down the hall, I heard Dylan's sobs: "No, NO, NO," he kept repeating while Ted stood tall, pushing the bathroom door open while his son was against the other side trying to shut it.

I wanted to gather information calmly, but one look at Ted's smirking face and I knew he was unreachable. So I yelled, "What are you doing, Ted?"

"*Me?*" He asked incredulously. "It's our son, Corinne! He is trying to shut the door!"

Upon realizing I was near, Dylan cried, "*Mama!*" and stepped away from the door, causing Ted to slip from the sudden lack of counterpressure. Dylan ran into my legs and was shaking all over, naked.

"Dylan? Are you okay? Did you throw up, honey? Is your stomach hurting?" I was confused.

"No, Tee wouldn't let me shut the door to do my poo-poo," Dylan cried out and fell into a heap of tears on the floor.

I hugged him, tears streaming down my face. One son was clinging onto my breast and the other's head was buried in my lap.

"Ted?" I asked.

"He's right. I don't think he should shut the bathroom door." He announced it as if it was a reasonable fact.

"No, Ted, he does get to. He is almost five now, and that is when privacy is important. Of course he gets to shut the door." I was beginning to feel dizzy and nauseous.

"No, he is too young, something could happen in there!" Ted was certain and adamant.

"He wasn't locking the door, right? Dylan, did you try to lock the door?" I rubbed his hair and he lifted his head. He looked at me with tear-filled eyes and shook his head. "No," he whispered.

"Ted, it is critical that he be allowed some privacy when he goes to the bathroom," I said. "In fact, come to think on it"—and in my pause an incredible rage overtook me, and I shouted, "I want to be able to go to the bathroom with the door shut too!"

In that moment, I realized that whenever I wanted to shut the door to the bathroom, he'd found an excuse to come in: he needed a tissue, he needed to wash his hands, or he needed to find something obscure under the sink like a sponge in the cleaning supply kit. Without realizing it, over the years, I'd just grown accustomed to not shutting the bathroom door.

He stared at me coldly for a few long seconds, then replied icily, "I don't know what you are talking about, Corinne."

I looked him right in his eyes and said, "Yes, you do! And it took me to see you doing it to Dylan to make me realize what you are doing! You are a sick bastard, Ted, really sick."

"Don't speak to me like that in front of our children." He grabbed my elbow hard and spit the words in my face.

Wiping my face dry with my spare arm, I cried uncontrollably while my son continued to breastfeed and my other one burrowed in my lap.

"Ted, you need some help. Please," I implored.

He looked away from me.

"Honey, look at us, we are your family," I begged as we sat huddled in a corner. "We need you healthy and you are not. Please stop this, Ted, we love you and we need you. This is about your father, Ted, I know it."

He remained silent and rigid.

"Ted, we love you," I was crying.

"I don't!" Dylan screamed and began punching Ted in his leg and thighs.

Ted grabbed his son's fists and shouted at him to stop. Dylan ran to my lap again, terrified.

"Ted, please, Ted, please please listen to me, you have a problem, and I am not even able to see it until you are mean to Dylan. Even then, whoa, I mean, I can't see you being mean until it is at him, oh MY GOD, maybe I have a problem for that!"

And I was lost in a scary void of confusion and wonder that can only be described as having the floor pulled right out from under you into a long, scary free-fall.

He stormed downstairs, muttering that we were not appreciating him, and turned on the television.

After going to the bathroom, Dylan crawled into my bed while I finished Colin's feed. He fell asleep as his little brother dozed off and I brought him to his own bedroom, newly painted with sharks and dolphins on the wall.

I went downstairs and watched television with Ted, feeling utterly alone and scared. We lived like zombies for the next six weeks until a recruiter called the home phone, out of the blue, with an opportunity for Ted to work in Boulder. Of course, Ted secured a job at this medical device start up. As a couple we had grown quite adept at promoting his career with my background in recruiting and his indisputable creativity and intelligence.

Driving down the hill into Boulder a week before Dylan's fifth birthday, late evening after a day of loading the moving trucks, I expected to feel excited and relieved. Instead I thought of a bizarre image in a book I'd read by Doris Lessing called *Descent into Hell*, and had dark visions.

Coming into Boulder, I couldn't help but notice the acres and acres of open space, undeveloped land that was left for the wildlife and that served to insulate the community from urban sprawl, a community secluded in a bubble, protected and nestled in the mountains, and I felt a chill run down my spine. Finding housing in Boulder had been difficult, something I'd never experienced. With great credit, a husband making over six figures and spotless references, we'd nonetheless been rejected by two landlords. One woman taking a sabbatical in New Zealand handed me back my application and told me she would keep looking; we weren't "a fit." "It's just this neighborhood is so, well, I don't know how to say this, the neighbors are, well, very Boulder." My only conclusion that my family and I were not so "very Boulder" and consequently would upset her neighbors. We wound up securing a house on the outskirts of town, in a development called Four Mile Creek, that eventually became known to me as Four Mile Shriek, as shrieking seemed to be my last resort in trying to get my husband to understand the severity of our problems.

As we drove on the freeway, I sang the bedtime song I'd created for my son, "Oh, Cooooolin, I love you,/You are as sweet as sweet can be, from your head down to your feet./Oh, Colin, I love you, you bring me happiness and joy, by being m-m-m-my little boy./Oh Colin, I love you." As I sang, my baby drifted slowly off to sleep in his car seat.

Dylan smiled and hugged his stuffed dinosaur, Baryonx. Ted was a few miles ahead, driving our minivan filled with fragile items I requested not to be put in the U-Haul.

Dylan whispered, "He is almost asleep, Mama."

I dropped my voice even lower. "Ohhhh, Cooolin, I love you, you have a kind and lo-ooo-ving heart and a brain so veeery smart."

Dylan giggled, "Mama! Is that a new one?"

I giggled quietly. "Yup, I used to do that for you too. I just made up new verses to keep me awake when I sang you the bedtime song."

Dylan seemed surprised that I had made the song up myself.

I told him that I had kept making up new verses while I was rocking him, looking at his adorable little baby face, and wondering why I could fall asleep in a heartbeat but his eyes would just stare at me totally wide open. When he was a baby, I told him, he would look at me for so long that I'd think I could fall asleep on a pillow made of concrete. "I was that tired being a new Mama," I said, "and you were still wide awake."

Dylan answered, "Because, Mama, don't you know? I had a lot of important things to tell you without words so I had to send them to you that way."

I paused, thinking deeply.

He continued, "Plus, Mama, the things I had to tell you are hard to say in words, so I had to be a baby to explain it all to you."

I looked at him in the rearview mirror, and asked, "Did I listen well?"

"Yes, Mama, you did, but there is still more, but Colin is telling you now, he knows it, I've forgotten most of it because I am so big!" He spoke with the assurance a young child has operating in these metaphysical fields.

I wanted to talk more on it but didn't, feeling it would taint something somehow. So I thanked him for telling me all that stuff while I was trying to get his cute little self to nap. "You must have had lots to say," I said, "because you'd want to rock for hours!"

He giggled, but then added in a tone of voice quite serious for a young boy, "Actually, Mama, I *did* have a lot to say!"

Then we dropped the conversation as he explained to me why Parasaralophus was his favorite dinosaur that week.

We had a six-month lease in Four Mile Shriek, and during that time, I begged for a marital separation and called therapists in a hysterical attempt to schedule him an appointment; but my pleas for help were ignored by both my husband and most of the professionals. I yelled, got migraines, couldn't get along with anyone in the home-schooling community and basically fell apart trying to show Ted that we had marital problems. He continued to respond in a cool and collected manner, requesting that I give our marriage the chance it never had and blaming all the stress in our life for our problems. My screams that we were making our own stress were left unanswered.

Our house in Monument wasn't selling so Ted's parents were paying the mortgage every month, to my dismay, and any attempts I made to problem-solve were in vain. One night while washing dishes, I suggested that we rent out the house. If his parents kept paying the mortgage, it was just going to de-value the property over time. No one would want to buy a house that had been on the market forever, I told him.

"You think you know everything, don't you?" Ted jeered at me before opening the refrigerator to look for a snack before bed.

"No, that is *not* it, Ted. I just think if your parents are paying the mortgage for much longer, it is a bad business decision." I was exhausted and my ever-present migraine was pounding.

"So, what do you think we should do, with all your infinite wisdom?" he asked.

I took my chance, hoping that for a change, my suggestions, my planning and my strategy could be incorporated into our lives. "I think we should ask your parents for a big loan against our stock, to be paid off upon IPO (the Initial Public Offering) in the neighborhood of say 10-20K, and that we should use that money to make the house the most desirable at that price point, making *anyone* look stupid for passing it up." I took a breath and paused.

He was silent.

I asked, "What do you think?"

He replied, "Nope."

His parents ended up dumping over roughly $40K into that house, paying the mortgage every month until we eventually had to foreclose over a year later.

My time in Four Mile Shriek was lost in a fog of exhaustion, childcare and excruciating migraines. My thoughts wandered about how to get out of the marriage: waiting until the lease was done would offer me a chance to separate, with Ted's eventual cooperation; but any conversation with Ted to troubleshoot separating domiciles, having two houses, splitting child-care schedules or soliciting professional assistance were either ignored or mocked. He'd call me "silly" and "ridiculous" or continue to blame my unhappiness on missing Massachusetts. He secured a loan from our financial broker in Colorado Springs, who found us a half-million-dollar mortgage to buy a house in Boulder. He knew about our current mortgage, but with Ted's parents' payments, we were afforded another mortgage with minimal interest. Tempted to consider beautiful houses along the Boulder Creek trail, I vacillated between a hope that settling in our own home would finally solve our problems and despair that nothing could save my marriage. After indulging Ted's many internet searches, weekend house touring and long convincing debates, I finally agreed to put an offer on a house on the bike trail for a beautiful half-a-million-dollar home. After our offer was accepted, however, I called the realtor in a panic, rescinding it at the last minute, much to Ted's befuddlement and anger. He claimed that my migraines were affecting my judgment, though he was relieved to avoid further financial debts. Throwing his arms up in disgust, Ted told me it was up to me to find our next house, and although I suggested two smaller houses instead and a marital separation, he said, in firmness, that under no set of circumstances would we be moving into anything but one house, all together as a family, the way it should be.

On my walks with the boys, I spotted some rentals around town and began to look inside the windows. One in particular excited me as it was modern, big and on the bike path. And, although pets were not allowed, I negotiated a higher rent, offered up pictures of myself, my pets and my children to the landlord in Germany, and through communications with the property management facility, secured a signed lease in June. And I knew that the bedroom in this house was mine and mine alone. As I unpacked and began to arrange the furniture, moving into this new house gave me a renewed strength and perspective. For the first time since living in Massachusetts, I was bringing out my decorations and comforting inessentials, like extra sweaters and candles.

One night, while lying in bed listening to Ted's snoring, I woke him up and asked him to leave the bed.

He grunted a response, only half awake.

"I want to sleep and you are keeping me up," I said, pushing him with my elbow.

He rolled over on his side and eventually I fell asleep, but the next day I asked him to put the spare mattress in the guest room, and since he refused, the following night I was more hostile and stubborn in my demand that he sleep elsewhere, swearing at him and being quite clear that a shared bed was no longer in our lives. From that night on, he dragged the mattress up from the basement every night to the living room, where he slept for four months, only to drag it downstairs again every morning before the boys woke up.

Late summer, I suggested that Ted take Dylan to Dinosaur National Monument for a fun summer camping trip. Ted had been complaining that I was getting in the way of his relationship with his son. Since I was breastfeeding, and the drive was so long, I felt this was a great chance for them to bond. Ted's excuses ranged from "the camping equipment is packed up" (I said we could unpack it) to "it's all old and moldy" (I suggested we take it out, see what we needed and buy a few sleeping bags if necessary) to "I can't take the time off of work." When I pointed out that he did so at least once each week for my migraines and if we pulled together and saved those days up, he could do a long weekend in August, he told me I'd never be able to go a week without him home from work. That made me feel deflated: my son couldn't go camping with his father at Dinosaur National Monument because of my weakness and migraines. And so, I suggested instead that they work on video-making, something Dylan was incredibly interested in. Ted showed mild interest in this, as his father was an amateur videomaker, and I wrote up scenes for them to shoot around Boulder. Wanting to see it to completion, Dylan requested each weekend that they go do some filming, but Ted sought perfection on the editing part, refusing to hear my requests to be less concerned with that and more focused on fun with his son. Instead, he expected Dylan to sit for hours next to him while he dabbled around on his Apple while mentioning frequently that in order to do the project properly he needed updated equipment. Dylan lost interest quickly.

I'd suggest they bike or play soccer during Colin's naps on the weekend, but Ted would come up with excuses, and then whine incessantly that I was making Dylan a Mama's boy. It began to dawn on me that Dylan's loyalty to me was what upset Ted the most. He had no idea how to ease his son into the world of men: a world of sports, fun and friendships. Dylan yelled "Go away, go away!" when Ted was home, and Ted responded with increased pouting and unhappiness that his son was turning against him. He took every opportunity to blame me for this discord.

The stress of living this way was taking its toll on my mothering and I felt like a walking zombie, going through the motions of making meals and enrolling Dylan in sports classes. I'd given up on trying to meet people.

On afternoon in August, I was feeling alienated from the Boulder community, a town where anything anyone could want was available, and yet, I had lost my enthusiasm and presented a hostile presence. As I watched two mothers chatting in the playground, I wanted to cry, missing so much having casual friendliness in my life, and I began thinking again about how to get Ted to move out. I couldn't argue with his position that our financial problems made the idea of dual households problematic. And yet having him drag the spare mattress up to the living room nightly was absurd. As I watched Colin climb and slide, I pondered options such as discontinuing my therapy, which could save us in roughly $500 a month, certainly enough to rent a place in someone's house. Or I imagined Ted moving back into our house in Monument and commuting to Boulder, an option he had proposed when we were living there, except in reverse. I began to imagine a career where I had my own office, but quickly my office became a bedroom and I wondered if my sons and myself could sleep in an office, which brought me to the chilling realization that I could not get Ted out of my life, and that no matter what I imagined, he would refuse, and I was stuck, miserable, unhealthy and unsupported. As I let this sink in, my focus went deep inside, and I heard a scream: Colin had been climbing, missed a step, and fallen.

I picked up my son as blood rolled down his chin. I put his head against my shirt as he cried in wails I'd never heard before. His tooth had broken through the skin of his lower lip.

Rushing the boys to Ted's office, I called him on my cell phone and frantically told him what happened. "Meet me at the doctor, we need to take him to the doctor!"

"It's all right," he said soothingly. "It's all right, he'll be fine, just come to the office."

Meeting me in the parking lot off to the side of his office, he was calm and I was hysterical. "It's all my fault!" I told him. "I wasn't paying attention!" I sobbed uncontrollably.

He examined Colin's chin, ignoring me.

While sobbing in the front seat, I commanded that Ted jump into the passenger seat so I could bring us to the pediatrician. Again, he ignored me.

"Ted, damn it, this is all my fault, I was thinking of what to do about *our lives* and how to *separate* and how to find the money for you to move out, and now look, our little Colin, oh my *God*, he got hurt because I was so distracted thinking about our pathetic and worthless marriage! My God, Ted, this is all because you won't *move out* and give me the separation I want! I was thinking about what to do, how to separate our houses, where to find the money and I realized how much a stubborn and selfish pig you are refusing to divorce me and, oh, Colin, oh, my God, I am sorry, Mama is so sorry!" I cried hysterically, feeling a pain in my chest.

"You stupid bitch, just shut up!" Ted's voice brought chills and instantly silenced me.

From the back seat, Dylan yelled "*Stop it!*" and started crying.

A man was walking to the car next to us, unknown to Ted, and heard the entire exchange. He looked at me as he got into his car, eyes locked on me the whole time, then looked at my children, and then to me again with pity. I stared at him, embarrassed and humiliated, wishing I could escape his stare, but there was nothing I could do except receive his look of wonder and pity.

I began to shake. I went to the back seat and hugged Dylan, who was crying in his car seat, until he calmed down. Going around the car to Colin's side as he sat whimpering in his little car seat, I told Ted I wanted to hug our baby, but he refused to move.

"I want to hug my son, Ted." I was crying again.

"He's *our* son, you bitch." Ted's eyes were glazed over.

"Ted, please, please," I cried. My desire to touch my son, to sooth him as he was bleeding, felt primal.

He slowly turned and used his large body to stand in my way. "Not until you say "our son," Corinne. He is *our* son."

Tears flowing down my cheek, with a knot in my throat, I whispered, "Okay, Ted, I want to hug our son."

He smirked at me, knowing how much I wanted to comfort our crying baby, who was looking at me with huge eyes. I tried to reach my hand around Ted's body to touch my baby, but he grabbed me on the wrists.

"Ted," I cried. "He needs me, he needs me to touch him and look, he's upset!"

Colin was crying now, and Dylan was crying again too, whispering, "Stop this, Mama, stop this, you can stop it, Mama, stop it, Mama it is up to you to make this go away."

I looked at Dylan, wondering if he blamed me for the fight, but in that moment, seeing both of my sons' red eyes as they whimpered, I realized that I was the only one to stop this for my family.

"Let's go," I ordered. "Ted, I need you home to help make sure Colin is okay."

I went into the driver's side and started up the car.

"Wait, Corinne, you can't order me around like that," Ted said. "I've got—"

I interrupted him. "Ted, today we are going to figure out how to separate and have two houses! I am done with this marriage. Why can't you *accept* that? We are going to figure it out, *today*, do you hear me?"

He slammed Colin's door, making him jump up in fright and begin crying again. Dylan rubbed his brother's arm.

"Another day missed at work," he mumbled. "See you at home."

My head was pounding. My migraines were continual now, night and day.

When we got home, the boys and I went into our reading room, filled with stuffed animals, a big leather chair, books and games.

I sat on the chair immediately to pull Colin into a feed. His bloody lip was still able to curl around my nipple, his eyes beginning to sleepily relax. Dylan pulled out his sketch book that I'd purchased in Colorado Springs. His drawings were a release for his feelings: his dinosaurs would cry, be angry and write me notes. Once he showed me his drawing of a Maisaura dinosaur, the "good mother lizard," playing with her babies with the word *Help!* above her head. Sharing his sketchbook with me was a way to communicate his feelings about our family's struggles; it made me listen to his increasingly urgent pleas to stop the pain. That day, he was drawing a big T-Rex with an open mouth, crying.

The minute Ted's car pulled up, the three of us tensed up, and Colin's dozing eyes fixed on me. He stormed into the house looking for us. Dylan brought his sketch book to my chair and sat between my feet.

"Okay, what do you have to say!" he barked at me over the child gate.

I whispered, "This is not good for the kids, Ted. We *need* a plan,"

"Like your safety plan?" he jeered at me.

Dylan pushed further into my legs and Colin kept dropping my nipple. Fixing my arm under my breast to support his feed, I continued, "No, Ted, we are way beyond my safety plan."

I'd made a plan for us to follow when things got heated, hoping to de-escalate our fights for the children's sake. I'd drawn up a chart with times in the evening, night and weekends and color-coded it according to who should leave the house and where they should go. For example, if a fight occurred during nap on Saturday or Sunday, Ted was supposed to go to the library until things cooled down. Either of us, ideally, should be able to cry "Safety plan!" and we'd have to just stop fighting and leave the house. He'd found it unfair, as mostly he was the one required to leave, but I assured him that was only because I was breastfeeding our sixteen-month-old son. At night, of course, it was he that was required to just go to a hotel should the fighting erupt. My plan never worked, and he would ignore me, call me ridiculous or just storm out of the room whenever I requested we use it.

"Are we, Corinne?" he said to me softly.

I told him that for the children's sake, we needed to separate. "What is going on is one hundred percent wrong," I said. "I mean, Dylan should be in school, Colin should be playing and you should be at work, and look at us: the kids are huddled around me, you are losing *more* time from work when we could be saving this time for fun family stuff, everything is a *mess*, and it has to *stop now*."

He stared at me.

"I have been telling you from as early as Dylan was Colin's age that this marriage is not going to work. I have begged you to get help professionally, and I am in therapy …"

He cut me off. "Yeah, lots of good that is doing," he said.

"It *is* doing good, actually. I think it is making me stronger. But that is what the problem is: you aren't letting me go!"

Colin's eyes were unmoving and fixed on my face. Dylan's arms were wrapped around my ankles, hugging my legs.

Ted looked at us and yelled, "You fucking cunt, look at you. You think you are a good mother, and look at this." He slammed his fist on the half wall separating the reading room from the hallway.

Colin pulled harder on my nipple, his little body now shaking uncontrollably. Dylan hid his head in my lap next to his brother. I stared out the window, for the first time noticing the leaves on the aspen trees.

"Look, there are yellow leaves," I said, absolutely traumatized.

"You are crazy!" he yelled, walking out of the room. And I believed him.

I told Dylan he had to move his head because I had to keep feeding Colin. I lifted my eldest son's head, noticing his eyes were huge and scared. "You can sit here again," I said. "Will you draw a picture?"

"No!" he said, but sat by my feet again.

I rubbed Colin's shaking body. The dried blood on his lip was starting to form a scab. "It's okay, sweetie," I said, and I began to sing them both our bedtime song, hoping it would offer some relief. I stared at the yellow leaves for awhile, settling myself down.

Just as we'd calmed down, Ted entered the room from the other side, the child gate no longer separating us. He sat on the ottoman across from us. Dylan pulled his legs in so that he made no physical contact with his father.

"Look," Ted said. "I'll go to therapy, if that is what you want. Okay?" He scratched his hair, and then continued, "And, I looked at your safety plan and I will take it seriously, Corinne, if it means we can stay together as a family, it's not a bad idea."

I said without thinking, "Yeah, remember? I used to be an intern at a shelter for battered women, and that is how I got the idea for my safety plan."

His anger erupted again, and he stood over me and his suckling son, put his middle finger in my face and yelled, "Fuck you!"

Dylan cried, "Stop it, stop it, stop it!" and ran to the living room to get pillows, then ran back and hit his father with them. Ted just laughed at him. Dylan continued and chased him around the house, while Colin shook again at my breast with fixed and unmoving eyes. I kissed his forehead, released his mouth, brought him to the window and showed him the yellow leaves on the aspen until he began to move his eyes in a more normal way; then I brought him a little stuffed horse to cuddle. I held him close as I went into the other room, wishing I could shield him from his brother's anger and his father's jest.

"You think that hurts?" Ted was saying to Dylan. "It doesn't. You can't hurt me."

I cried out for Ted to stop. "He just a boy," I said. "My God, Ted, he's your son!" I called Dylan over to me, but he kept hitting his father over and over with the pillows while Ted laughed at him.

"I don't have to put up with this," Ted said as he reached for his jacket and walked towards the garage door. "I'm going to the office."

I felt instantly relieved, and Colin's body softened. But Dylan followed Ted to the garage door with the pillows. Colin began crying so I took him to the reading room, and picked up a book about a bear.

"Look, Colin, bear is on his bike." Colin sat stiffly, looking at the pictures. "See, he hops on his bike and where does he go?" I tried to keep my voice as cheerful and normal as possible. "Yes, he goes to the beach!! Now, where does he go?"

And I heard the garage door slam shut.

"Dylan?" I hoped Ted was gone and Dylan would come into the reading room to join us.

I turned another page of the book, but Dylan didn't come in.

"Shit!" I dropped the book and ran to the garage with Colin in my arms.

Opening the garage door, I saw Ted pulling Dylan's arm and lifting him by his wrist above the air while his feet dangled. He brought his son's face up to his and said sternly, "You had better stop it *now.*"

Time slowed for me in a way that it never had before. Dylan's terrified face stared at me. Colin's body shook in my arms.

Our snow shovel was next to me, right by the steps, ready and waiting. I looked at Dylan, flashed for a moment to his birth and saw how little and soft and innocent he was. Then I looked at his father, holding his son up, feet dangling to reach the floor, while he sobbed, terrified, begging to be released. And the snow shovel, within arm's reach.

My eyes darted from my son, to my husband, to the shovel, to my baby, to the shovel, to my son—still desperately trying to reach his feet to the ground while his father held him up, laughing—to the shovel, to my baby, to my husband's head turned away from me, to my baby, to the snow shovel, to my son, to my husband.

I reached over and pressed the garage door opener, just above the shovel. As the door eased up, Ted immediately dropped Dylan, who fell in a heap on the ground sobbing, and the neighbor across the lane, smoking a cigarette while examining his tree's leaves, looked over. Ted waved at him and got a head nod in return.

"Okay, hope you feel better," Ted said to Dylan as he opened the door to the minivan.

I gathered Dylan in my arms while holding Colin and said, "Okay boys, let's go have lunch."

As we entered the house, I held them both in a big hug and whispered, "It will get better. It will."

We continued on with their nap and our usual routine, and when Ted got home that afternoon, we were in the reading room playing "Fly to the planets." Dylan was pretending to be an astronaut while I read to him about the various planets. Colin was walking around the room with us, saying, "Me too." We were learning about the solar system.

Once Ted arrived, Dylan stopped playing and Colin crawled into my lap.

"What's wrong?" I asked, not realizing the adult mind's capacity to compartmentalize trauma was quite different from that of a child.

Neither son answered, but sat clinging to me while their father sat on the leather chair. I truly had "forgotten" the earlier incident, and was unable to access it.

"I called a therapist today," Ted said.

The memory of the morning's events came flooding in and I pulled my children in closer.

"Good," I said.

"And we can do the safety plan, if that helps," he said.

"Okay," I responded. "I'll go make dinner."

And, after a meal of spaghetti and broccoli, I set about doing bedtime with the boys. Dylan refused to take a shower or a bath, wanting to be with me the entire time I soothed Colin down. Eventually both boys were in bed.

My head pounding, and feeling completely depleted, I went downstairs to make some tea. Ted had pulled the spare mattress up from the basement and was already in his pajamas. I knew I'd have insomnia that night, and was caught in a cycle of anxiety, exhaustion and trauma. I left a message for my therapist for an emergency session the next evening and went to boil some water. Ted followed me into the kitchen. He opened the refrigerator, and then sat down at the table. I put a tea bag in my cup, and began crying.

"Are you okay?" he asked.

"No, Ted, I'm not," I said, crying harder now. "I cannot believe our family. I mean, my God, what are we going to do?" My head and the muscles of my neck ached, and my stomach felt knotted, "We are failing our sons, Ted, failing them in everything we are doing,"

He stopped my vent, "No, you are a fantastic mother, look at all you do with them, the learning and the activities, and you give them everything they need."

I wondered if he could be so naïve, that the fighting, the pain and the trauma were just not in his conscious reality.

"We have a plan, Corinne, therapy and your safety plan. It's a good idea." He seemed hopeful and I had that familiar feeling of guilt for not believing in any future with him.

"Yeah, I suppose." I poured the hot water into my cup and sat down at the table. I put my head on the dirty placemat, with dried noodles from dinner, and cried. When I lifted my head, a piece of spaghetti was on my forehead. Ted reached over and gently took it off.

"Can I ask you a question?" He looked at me.

I nodded and took a sip of my tea.

"Do you like it here in Boulder?" He seemed concerned.

"I don't know," I said. "I am too worried about our family to think on it." I stood up to get an ice cube for my tea, deciding to stay standing by the counter instead of returning to the table.

"Well, it's just that, you know, Boulder has been hard for us," Ted said.

I was quiet and tired. I told him that I thought of Massachusetts sometimes, and I knew that we had a chance there to do things right for our family, but we had missed our chance. We had been starting out our lives and had so many opportunities for success, and we just messed up and missed the chance to have a healthy thing going on. I began to cry, and he stood up and put his arms around my shoulders.

"It's like all we did was complain," I said, "and yet, I had so much fun there with Dylan, play dates, skating on the pond, the farms. It was nice, you know? And, now I am just so upset all the time." I cried harder.

Ted gently turned me around so I could face him, then he stepped back a bit. "You know, Corinne, you were better in Massachusetts. More yourself!"

I stopped crying and laughed sarcastically. "Don't you remember, Ted? You were all about telling me I was more myself in California! You said I was depressed in Massachusetts, but I think it was our marriage that made me so depressed. I wanted to divorce."

He shuddered in pain and whispered, "I know."

"Ted, this has never been about you," I said. "It's always been about *us*. Since having Dylan, I knew that we couldn't do this right for him married. That's why I wanted a divorce—not to hurt you. I wanted a divorce so that we could be the best parents we could be for Dylan, and now Colin. And that is truly apart. Don't you see that?"

He stood stony and silent.

"It's like we have to put *our* pain aside so we can focus on *them*. Let's not do this anymore, Ted, please."

He paused. "It's moving so much," he said. "It's run havoc on our marriage, and now being in Boulder, this place isn't right for us. We thought it was, but it's not. It's like running into my sister and mother all the time."

I flinched when he said that, and asked him what he meant.

"It's like people here think they are better than everyone else," he said. "The entitlement!" He was becoming quite talkative now. "They project all their anger onto others, think they are perfect and then act like they deserve everything. Just look around: the town is isolated and secluded and angry, filled with righteous and angry people. I mean, even you noticed it when you got here. You said people were too serious. You said you never heard laughter."

I was surprised that he had paid attention to my initial observations about Boulder and even more curious about why he had mentioned his sister and mother.

"Like your mother?" I asked.

"Yeah, I mean hiding behind perfect and then acting like nothing is right with anyone else," he said. "It makes me sick to live here!"

I looked at him, wondering if he had a type of post-traumatic response to living in Boulder, as I could certainly see the parallels between his family and aspects of the community. I mentioned the time I had been chastised at the library for having Colin in a stroller and not a bjorn. Colin was such a big child, and unable to fit anymore in my snuggly carrier, when a girl told me her mother said that a bjorn made your baby feel more loved, and mothers who put their children in strollers weren't doing things right. He mother, hair in braids, wore a long flowing hemp skirt and carried a small baby in a bjorn while looking for books. I stood with my hands on the stroller, balancing Dylan's dinosaur atlas on the top while Colin played with a plastic toy. I had responded sarcastically to the pre-teen, "You know, if your mother thinks love is about a baby-carrier, then, sweetie, she has a lot to learn." And I left in a huff, feeling her condescending stare.

"Exactly!" Ted was animated. "I mean where on earth would someone get away with a comment like that except here in Boulder, the land of the righteous?"

I told him there were people like that everywhere, and even he had said that his own family was like that. "Remember your sister being so upset that we weren't using cloth diapers?" I asked.

He agreed, but he said that there were so *many* of them in Boulder; the city was like a magnet for people who thought they were better than everyone else.

He was right. Even my therapist had called Boulder "the town of angry nice people," and he'd lived there for over a decade. "What can we do, though?" I asked. "We have no money, the house in Monument isn't selling, the boys are upset, but yes, if what you are asking is, 'Do you miss New England?' I say a true and real and emphatic 'Absolutely, I miss it every day, I have New England nostalgia every day.' But there isn't a damn thing I can do about it. We are living in Boulder, and no, truth be told, it is nothing of what I thought and filled with hypocrisy, and people thinking they are so evolved and yes, I could go on, but what bothers me night and day, and what I really want is for our family to stop hurting so much and to be healthy!" I sunk into the counter, missed the ledge and almost fell.

He reached out to try to catch me, but I'd regained my balance quickly.

He reminded me of the fun I'd had in Massachusetts, trying to soothe me as I cried. I whispered, "We had the beginnings of it all there, Ted, and you missed my warnings."

"I know," he said gently. "I should have listened to you, but I didn't."

We were standing close, in a comfortable way.

"We lost our chance, Ted," I said. "We had a chance and it is gone."

Tears rolled down my cheeks, making it impossible to see. I couldn't wipe them away fast enough.

"Maybe not," he said. "Maybe we haven't missed our chance." Ted left the kitchen briefly to get me a Kleenex from the bathroom. He handed it to me and said, "Let's try to get back there, but let's go together, okay?" He held out his arms for a hug.

"How?" I asked, standing still against the counter, not entering his arms.

He said that our stock would come to IPO soon, and we just had to hold onto those future funds and in that way, we'd get back east. He seemed confident.

I told him that I had written in my journal just after leaving Massachusetts that this was a three-year cycle, and we'd either get back to Massachusetts together or we'd end up divorced. He laughed sincerely about my ability to predict the future, genuinely impressed over the years with this talent of mine. "If you say three years is up soon," he said, "then yahoo, our stock is coming up soon."

As I reminded him that this winter was three years for the marital prediction, I mentioned that the stock becoming IPO flashed me a number five but that was utterly unrelated to our marriage cycle, which ended this March precisely; the clarity of my knowledge surprised me. Later our stock would open at an initial public offering in May for $15/share. I looked up at his blue eyes, now so kindly regarding me. And, this time when he opened his arms for a hug, I walked to him, put my head on his chest, and breathed in the familiarity of his smell, offering me comfort and contentment.

I whispered, "But Ted, when are we going to stop trying to get to 'there' and start being content with 'here,' wherever that is? I want us to be comfortable in the 'here'."

My question hung in the air as we hugged. Then I released, finished my tea, and went up to bed, looking down the banister at him as he pulled the comforter up over himself, lying on the spare mattress on the living room floor. A wave of guilt came over me that my husband was not allowed to sleep in my bedroom. But it passed as quickly as it came up.

"Good night," I called.

"We'll make it," he said. "We will get back to Massachusetts together. Good night!"

He turned over, grabbed the extra pillow and tucked it under his arm in a hug.

After deciding to skip my tooth brushing, I crawled into bed and cried for forty-five minutes, hoping that Ted was right and that somehow we'd save our marriage before the three-year cycle ended in just over six months. Colin called me for his night-time feed, ending my opportunity to cry and we both eventually fell asleep in the big king-sized bed, cozy and cuddling. He had learned to feed without waking up and his lip was already scabbed over.

The following week, Ted had found a therapist he loved, a man who encouraged him to play hockey again, and, according to Ted, felt that I was too controlling. He told Ted he needed to assert himself and connect deeply with his masculinity. Ted joined a recreational team with no problem, but I requested that if I should get one of my migraines, he stay home to help with the dinner or bedtime routine. He huffed and rolled his eyes, insulted. He would never prioritize hockey over his family, he said, and agreed that on those evenings when I was overwhlemed he would stay home.

After a long day, with only three hours of sleep for five nights straight, I was dizzy and sick to my stomach, and breastfeeding Colin actually hurt, I was so tired. I requested that Ted do bedtime so I could get to bed early.

He responded by telling me he had an important game and he needed to go.

I was clearing up the dinner dishes while Colin was smearing spaghetti around his high chair. Dylan's face pinched as he left the table, snuck up to his room and shut the door.

"Play-offs, already? I thought the season just started," I said, rubbing my temples and leaning against the counter for support.

"It did," he said, "but I am making my mark on the team. I can't just not show up to a game." He stood up, leaving his dishes on the table.

As I picked up the large Creuset pot to bring it to the sink and wash, it slipped out of my hands and banged onto the floor. I told Ted I was exhausted—even lifting that pot was too much. "I realize you love hockey," I said, "but our family is in crisis, and emotional chaos, and I don't understand how this can be so important."

His shoulders caved in, stomped his foot on the ground and muttered that I was unreasonable.

I suggested he call the captain, as being a father himself, likely he'd understand a last-minute change in plans. Leaving the dirty Creuset pot on the stove, I began loading the dishwasher with lighter items while he sat back down at the table with a big sigh.

"No, Corinne, I can't," Ted said sternly and stood up.

Respecting that maybe his therapist's suggestion that he play hockey might fix our problems, as impossible as it was to believe, I let it go. As I put soap in the dishwasher, I quietly agreed to his game that night, and wondered how I would find the energy to walk up the stairs, let alone get my sons to bed.

His only chore in the kitchen was to take out the recycling and garbage, both of which piled up each week, attracting fruit flies. I would let the mess pile up, then either take it out myself or request that he do his part in cleaning up.

As I looked at the Creuset pot on the stove, knowing that the spaghetti would crust overnight, I couldn't imagine cleaning it; the task seemed too daunting.

Before gathering Colin in my arms to take a bath, I asked Ted to take out the recycling on his way to his game.

"Don't talk to me like that!" he said, slamming his fist on the kitchen table. "Hey, where's my hockey jersey?" He stood up as if nothing happened.

I put Colin back into the high chair, knowing that a fight was eminent.

"In the basket, cleaned, like always," I muttered, then yelled, "You know you aren't in the NHL last time I checked, and it would be wonderful to have some help tonight. I have a splitting headache, dammit; even my jaw is aching. I haven't slept more than three hours a night in almost a week!"

His feet pounded the stairs as he went in search of his hockey jersey. I watched Colin make circles with spaghetti sauce on his tray, realizing that I had to eventually summon the strength to pull him out and bring him to his bath.

I began crying and immediately got scared that I wouldn't be able to stop crying ever, so I yelled at my husband sarcastically instead, "You're not Gretszky last time I checked, Ted, and, even he could balance fatherhood with an NHL career. I mean, his wife was clearly a happy woman. Did you ever see the way she looked at him?"

He was in my face before I could blink, with a finger pointed at my forehead, screaming at me that he was a man, and I was destroying his life and that even his therapist agreed I was a fuck-up. A tirade of words assaulted me as my eyes fixed on our baby playing with his spaghetti.

I slipped out from under his wrath and got a pile of boxes, newspapers and cans from the recycle pile. "Will ya at least take these to the can on your way out, being that you are such a manly man now?"

He grabbed them out of my hands, scratching my arm as he did, letting half of them fall to the floor. "See you later," he grunted.

"Not looking forward to it," I growled back. "Don't hurry back. In fact, don't come back!"

He called me a bitch and said "fuck you" on his way out, so I followed him to the garage, crying that he shouldn't talk to me like that in front of our children. I slammed the door shut behind him. Immediately, he opened the door, scattering the recycling items on the garage floor. My stomach turned and my eyes darted to Colin in his high-chair. I began to push the door back shut as he opened it, calling me an ungrateful and worthless bitch. I repeated over and over, "Just go, would you, go already!" But he was stuck, eyes locked on me in rage. He was using his entire strength to push the door open, while I had nudged my foot against the wall behind me, using my entire body and the wall to make sure he couldn't get through the few inches of space he was trying to make bigger.

"Open this door, you stupid bitch!" his face red and his knuckles white.

"No, just go, Ted, please, just go!" I was crying hysterically, my foot bruising against the wall and adjusting my balance in pain. He seized the opportunity to push harder, his hand now wrapped around the door.

"You have no right kicking me out of my house, the house I pay rent for you lousy mooch! Now open this door!" He dug his foot into the floor and anchored it, making it even harder for me to push shut.

I countered his force, amazed at my physical strength. "Ted, I am sorry, just go, please, go play hockey."

As he pushed the door open, I flashed to a memory of our dating period, when I'd been watching one of his recreational hockey games, and was talking with the wife of another player. She had commented on Ted's anger, saying that it gave her chills. Where the other players resigned themselves to a penalty, she noted, he stayed angry throughout his time-out, and she felt that he showed the signs of a serious anger management issue, taking the entire game much more personally than the others. I'd joked that all the players fantasized that they were NHL players instead of Silicon Valley nerds on a recreational team, but she'd looked at me with a long look, and said, "No, there is something different about him." I had stopped talking to her from that moment on.

As Ted was able to open the door wider and wider, I lost my strength, and finally let the door open, exhausted and resigned. He put his face only inches from mine and snarled long and loud, then spit right into my face. The splash of saliva shocked me, and I felt dinner turn in my stomach. I looked at him, the ugliest man I've ever known, and said, "Don't ever do that again, you bastard!"

Colin began crying, and Dylan cried a pain-filled call to me from the stairs, witness to the entire event. I faced my sons, their four eyes searching me, trying to hold onto something secure, and the intensity of their stares was unbearable. So I returned to the kitchen staring at the ground, my neck tense, and wiped my face off with a napkin.

Ted left immediately, as if he had done nothing wrong, and Dylan sat on the floor in silence with his hand in mine while I using the other one to wash his brother whom I'd managed to gather the strength to carry to a warm bubble bath.

Hours later, long after the boys had fallen asleep, Ted walked in smelling sweaty, said "We won," and went into the shower.

After his shower, he walked out of the downstairs bathroom and opened the basement door to get the spare mattress.

"No, Ted, no," I said. "You are not sleeping here tonight. I cannot sleep with you in the house. We have to do our safety plan!"

"Ha! I don't know what you think you mean, Corinne, bossing me around like that, but *yes* I can sleep here and *yes* I will sleep here." He opened the basement door, dragged up the mattress and dropped it on the living room rug, amid Legos and Fisher Price toys.

I was crying into a pillow, unable to look at him. "Please, Ted, this isn't about anything, at all, it isn't, it is about you just going so we can *all* sleep. I cannot sleep with you here. I mean, you *spit* on me tonight! I will never settle down with you in the house, and I need to sleep to take care of the boys tomorrow, I haven't slept well in…. years! Please, please, please, hear me for once!"

I sobbed into the pillows, not able to raise my head.

"Then *you* leave," he said. "I am sleeping right here." And I heard him pat the mattress and fluff up his pillow and make it clear he was covering himself with a blanket.

"Ted! I would, but *I am breastfeeding Colin!*" I was floored by his insensitivity. "Otherwise, yes, I would go, the boys are asleep."

Lifting my head, I saw he'd crawled into his bed, was reading his book and pretending he couldn't hear me. I came downstairs and grabbed his book, threw it across the room and told him to go to hell.

"Just shut up and go to sleep," he said. "It's not my problem you have insomnia!" He closed his eyes and asked me to shut off the light on my way upstairs.

It had been a day from hell, including spaghetti, spit and a migraine, and even though the trauma had begun to numb me to my sons' experiences, I certainly knew they lived in hell with me and wanted me to save them.

"I have insomnia because I am married to *you*! Now, go!" I pulled the pillow out from under his head.

He grabbed it roughly, put it back, turned his back to me and pretended to sleep.

"You're not leaving tonight, are you?" I whispered.

"Nope!"

I considered calling 911, as I had in the past, hanging up before an answer, but put the phone away, not sure what they would do to help me in this situation. Ted called me a coward.

I woke up Dylan and Colin at 1:30 a.m., put them in the car, and drove to a hotel in town. I arranged the furniture to ensure Colin wouldn't roll out of the bed, made the spare bed into a sleeper for Dylan and put my children to sleep. I cried for an hour, quietly, wishing I never had to see my husband again. When we got home the next morning, he was already at work.

Saturday night he had another hockey game, and my resentment was uncontrollable. I told Ted his therapist was a moron to tell him the answer to our problems was to play hockey, and that a real man is nice to a woman and loves his wife instead of pretending to be a jock. Colin was crawling around the floor picking up various toys while Dylan was overly focused on building a Lego truck.

"He thinks I need to reconnect with my masculinity and that you are controlling me," he said triumphantly, smiling a sardonic smile. "And, there isn't a damn thing you can do. He's onto your games of control and dominance, and he is going to help me with you. He knows what you are doing to me!"

I put my head on the table and cried.

"I just want some time for myself once in awhile," I whispered, "and our lives are such a mess. You can't do this, keep going to hockey like it's therapeutic, while we are getting *no*where. Damn it," I said to myself, "all I want is to divorce. I want to divorce and all my husband can do is make it out like I am crazy. I am not crazy, I am just married to an asshole!" I picked up a glass of water on the table and walked towards the sink.

Ted walked over to me in a rush, his red angry face in mine, his big nose pressed into mine, and he pushed me against the wall. "You will *never* say that again in front of our children, you bitch!" He spit in my face again, less shocking the second time around. I wiped my cheek against my shoulder to clean the saliva off. Immediately, he held my shoulders against the wall. "This is what my therapist is talking about! You are controlling me!"

I laughed, a true and genuine laugh, and said, "Look at yourself, you freak, you are holding me up against a wall saying that I am controlling! You are an absolute freak! You are sick and disturbed, the most disgusting individual I have ever met! Now if you wouldn't mind, I'd like to leave a message with your therapist about you holding me against a wall, spitting on my face, and accusing me of being controlling." My laughter turned hysterical.

Stunned, he stepped back and put his hands in his pockets.

I lifted the glass in my hand, splashed it in his face and said, "Would you please stop spitting on me, it is really vile. What's your therapist's number? I'd like to ask him what he thinks about my request to divorce you? You know, you freak, that request I made when Dylan was less than 18 months old? What does he think about your inability to divorce like a normal man? Does he suggest joining a basketball league?"

"We don't talk about it," Ted said, eyes locked on mine. "I never told him you wanted a divorce."

Picking up the nut plate off the counter, I mocked him. "Right, that would be, well, a normal conversation a *man* would have with a therapist, let's see, along the lines of 'Hey therapist, my wife doesn't want to be married, I am acting like a freak, scaring my sons, hurting my family, could you help me?'"

As I passed him to walk to the sink, he grabbed my elbow. "What? You gonna throw that at me?"

"*No*, Ted." I put the plate on the nearby counter, "I am not!" I talked again in my regular voice, the mockery gone. "I'm going to put it in the sink. Let go of my arm!"

"Awww, c'mon, Corinne," he jeered. "You are mad, aren't you?" He swung my arm around like a jump rope.

"Yes, Ted." I said, "I am really angry, but not because you are being an immature loser right now, because you won't divorce me like a normal person and cooperate in raising our sons in a healthy way. That is what's killing me, Ted, your sickness!"

He put his finger on my temple. "Aww, c'mon, you know you want to pick up that plate and just throw it at me, c'mon." He lifted my chin so I looked right in his eyes, full of hate and anger.

I picked up the plate, screamed in rage, and threw it in the sink, where it shattered. Colin cried and Dylan came running over, yelling, "I hate you," and hitting Ted with pillows. I scooped Colin in my arms, pulled Dylan away from his father and took the boys up to put them to bed.

By the time I had returned to the kitchen to clean the mess, Ted was long gone to his hockey game.

That following weekend, the first weekend in October, I suggested that Ted take the boys pumpkin picking at a local farm, affording me a few hours to myself, something I hadn't had in over six months. He put it off until Sunday afternoon, begging me all weekend to make it a family event; but when I kept refusing, he finally had no choice except to go with the boys by himself.

On his way to the farm, a fifteen-minute drive, he called me three times on the cell phone asking me if I'd changed my mind, mentioning to me yet again that this would be such a good time to bond as a family. Eventually, I let the answering machine field his calls and continued working on a short story that had been brewing inside for months.

At the farm, he called a fourth time and I finally answered, unable to concentrate on my writing with all the interruptions.

"Corinne, you have to see this and I can tell that the boys miss you and want you to be here. This farm is exactly like the ones you went to in New England. You'd love it. You have to come."

I refused, saying that I needed some time, and that the boys were fine without me for an hour or so. He kept insisting I come. He told me there were animals, hay rides, and a maze. It was exactly what I missed about New England.

"Dylan is asking for you," he said, "and I think Colin may need a feed while we are here. You have to come. The boys need you here. And I do too," he added. "It can help you see what we are going back to.... . Remember all those good times we had in Massachusetts?"

I sighed and looked around our house, missing what were easier and cozier times in Massachusetts, where my marital problems lay comfortably on the spectrum of normal. I closed my eyes, bringing myself back in time where I was just a typical dissatisfied wife complaining about her husband's short-comings. And, I enjoyed being in that place where our occasional fights about in-laws, parenting responsibilites and household chores were easily dismissed the next day. In Massachusetts, I had the luxury of illusion and many comfortable veils to hide behind; perfect parenting, false images of marital bliss, criticizing others instead of looking at myself, and honoring Ted as a good provider rather than expecting a partner. An unbearable feeling of nostalgia overcame me, and I felt an amazingly deep bitterness that I'd lost the luxuries of manipulating perceptions, and that I could no longer manage marital dissatisfaction like so many others. In my haste and upset, I'd challenged our attempt to settle into domestic roles, I refused to be a dissatisfied stay-at-home mother having boring sex, being supported financially, upset by my husband's laziness, and couldn't just settle into some normal dysfunction called marriage. I'd pushed it by moving to California, leaving Ted behind, complaining to divorce attorneys, and by expecting more from my husband and from myself. I wanted true partnership, good sex, harmonious living and a purposeful, well-planned-out life. The functional dysfunction, where so many live, was abhorrent to me, and I couldn't just be Ted's wife, Dylan's mother, happily unhappy, a woman without identity. I sat on the floor and cried, mad at myself for not settling into a lifestyle pretending everything was all right. If only I'd figured out a way to have settled into this humdrum lifestyle, and home schooled my children without worrying about their social life, not cared that I had no connection to community, stayed bitter, gossiped about the neighbor's problems and faked orgasms instead of wanting my sons to see real love; if only I could have done all of that, Ted would have never turned rancid on me. I cried for him. I cried for me. And, I cried for our sons.

Picking up the phone, I told Ted I'd meet them at the farm in twenty minutes.

At dinner that night, I was silent, just nodding or shrugging in response to every question Ted asked. Nervously, he asked if the farm had upset me. I replied that I was upset that I couldn't get an hour to myself whereas he got to go to hockey twice a week, and that it was critical I be able to have some down time for myself. I added that he should spend more time with his sons.

"Don't tell me how to be a father for my sons," he growled, "I am a great father to these boys."

I laughed. "Are you really proud of yourself as their father?" I asked. "I mean, do you get up in the morning feeling good about the way you treat your family?"

I got up and went to my room until dinner was finished, came down to take care of the dishes, did bedtime with my sons, and retreated into my office to do an internet search on narcissist personality disorders.

So much anger, so much discord: pages and pages of people outraged at their partners' behaviors. I'd had enough, and went downstairs to boil water for a cup of tea.

As the kettle warmed on the stove, I looked through the pictures in our digital camera from that afternoon; we seemed a normal and happy family in a pumpkin patch, no different than anyone else. Wandering back to the kitchen, I wondered how many others had problems like ours behind closed doors. That's when I noticed that Ted was standing by the cabinet, muttering, "Dumb *bitch*! Who does she think I am? Narcissism my ass? She's a freak! She is a freak, not *me*. She's is the one with all the problems. Narcissist? Ha!"

I realized that I'd left the computer screen on the site I had researched. In my exhaustion, I had neglected to cover my tracks. As he mumbled and swore about me in a manner that reminded me of Rain Man, I tried to get a cup out of the cabinet but he was in the way.

"Why don't you say it to my face, huh? You lousy bitch, just say it to my face," he said. "Narcissist?"

"Look, Ted," I said, "it isn't a big deal. Geez, according to all that, I am likely borderline, depressed or something like that, or I was when we met. I don't feel like it so much anymore, but all I am trying to do is figure out our problems." I tried to lighten the mood. "I just want answers to why we are hurting so much and can't have a normal divorce!"

"Yeah, well, you said it, not *me*."

I told him that I had come to accept that he had married a woman with lots of childhood wounds, one of which was to take on others' problems as her own, but that, along the way, I was healing, wanting a new way for my sons, and I explained that my sons deserved the best mother I could be, which meant being honest about the manipulations, control and nasty anger in our marriage. As a result, I had seen him get sicker over the years. I said I wanted to consider people more gently and less critically, make friendships, negotiate a visiting schedule with his family of origin, be a part of my community, have a meaningful career, budget our finances for longer-term planning, strategize our lives to avoid chaos and try to guide our sons through tough challenges instead of living life in denial, dysfunction and creatively covering it all up. But all he could do through my transformation was the craziest mind-fuck I'd ever seen and in truth, he was totally and truly unreachable and unethical, and there was not a psychological label for someone so mean he'd hold his wife hostage in marriage and using her sons as bondage. I told him that I felt sorry for him, because over the years my healing had made him crazy, because me being crazy had made him feel sane, and that he was truly the most disturbed individual, devious, mean and ruthless, that I'd ever met.

He stepped aside and I refused to look at his face, knowing I'd hurt him, or, quite possibly, had stunned him with my candid accuracy about his agenda. Before the inevitable onslaught of anger his face sometimes showed so much pain that it cut me to my core. I opened the cabinet for my cup.

"You are a cunt," he said, "a good for nothing bitch, and everyone knows it: your mother, my mother, everyone. My therapist even says you are messed up!"

I laughed. "Yup, messed up to be married to you. Sadly, Ted, we both had some big problems psychologically or we wouldn't be in this situation, but you see, I am trying to get us out, I am crying out for help, and you are just being meaner and more controlling with each and every passing day."

And I poured the water in my tea cup and turned to exit the kitchen, he grabbed my arm, spilling hot water on my wrist.

"Ouch, Ted, *stop it*!" I pulled my arm away and walked out of the room.

He followed me, yelling, "You bitch! You ungrateful lousy bitch! I do every-thing for you and you do nothing. How do you think you have money to eat? *Me!* How do you think you have a bed to sleep in? *Me!* How do you think you can buy everything that you do? *Me!*" He followed me to the hallway.

"Please be quiet," I said, "I don't want to wake the boys." I sat on the bench in our living room.

"*I don't give a damn!*" he yelled, and I imagined having to go to a hotel again that night.

"Ted, your anger, it is so scary, please stop!" I put my tea cup down as my hands had begun to shake.

"You are crazy, Corinne, you know that? Crazy, crazy, crazy crazy!" He was storming around the living room in circles, repeating over and over.

The camera was on the counter next to my calendar. I got it, walked over to him and told him he needed to see himself when he was like this. "You just don't know how you get!" I said, and I began video-taping him with the special two-minute video function.

He rushed over to me and forcefully grabbed the camera out of my hands, his fist splitting my lip open. I felt blood pouring down my chin.

"Oh my *God*, Corinne!" He sat on the couch in a slump, shocked at his behavior. "Corinne, I am so sorry!" He began to cry.

I ran to the mirror and saw an image of a woman with her hair disheveled, lip bleeding and eyes puffy, an image no woman should ever have facing her in the mirror. I picked up the phone and called 911.

"Don't do this," Ted pleaded as I dialed. "The boys. Think of the boys, your sons, think of Colin and of Dylan, my God, what are you doing? This will ruin their lives! Think about your sons for a moment. Don't react, Corinne. Please, please, don't react to this, you are too reactive, think of the boys!"

In a hard and sad voice, I whispered, "I *am* thinking of my sons, Ted, and it is for them that I do this." Then the emergency operator got on the phone to take down my contact information.

Sitting on the stairs, feeling the blood drip into my mouth, I understood the enormity of the opportunity I was taking, and sat in a vast emptiness knowing my life and my sons' lives were changing forever. With one simple phone call for help, I'd made a decision for my whole family, an action that would change the course of all of our lives, and there is truly no way to describe that stillness nor to honor its magnificence in my life. After years of pleading, begging and hoping for changes, the only way out of this marraige was to call the police. I didn't make Ted split my lip, of course not, but I knew I was taking advantage of a situation to end this living hell for once and for all, and as easily as I could excuse him for this 'mistake' or see his behavior as accidental, as likely it was, I knew that I had to call the police, get help, not let this get worse for the betterment of my sons' lives and mine, and really, and truly, for my husband's life too.

After twenty minutes, the police handcuffed my husband and charged him with third-degree assault. He'd shown absolutely no remorse when they talked to him. In fact, he blamed me the entire time, and tried to convince them to arrest me instead. My insides felt hollow. As he was escorted out of the house, turning on his way out to look at me with absolute hatred, the police officer turned him back around and walked him out the door. Once the door was shut, I collapsed on the floor and buried my head in my lap, only to have the victim hotline call me. After assuring them I was fine, I cried until Colin's three a.m. feed. That entire night I lay in bed, watching the moon shining brightly in my window, illuminating my pillow. Our house was still. Drifting off to sleep, memories of our better times flooded in. Ted had said, "We'll have our problems, Corinne, no doubt. But we'll learn together and grow." Words from a man I'd lost the moment I put on my gold ring, a man who stopped kissing me on my wedding night, a man who threatened to take my six-month-old-son away from me, a man I doubted existed after spending wasted years looking for him. I crawled out of bed—literally—inching across the floor on my knees, found my nature ring in my jewelry box, and slipped in on my pinkie. I missed Ted. I wished I had him as I had once known him. I wondered how I would make it through this with my sons. I walked into Dylan's room. His angelic face was peaceful against his pillow, and he held his Baroynx dinosaur under his arms. I kissed his cheek—my son, my beautiful and innocent son, angry and hurting, and relying on me. I stood above Colin's crib, holding my sobs in silence, my baby born into violence, hatred and fear, my son, innocent and as lost as I. I reached in and touched his hand, and wondered how I would ever be able to heal his infant wounds. Finally, I collapsed into my bed and buried my head in my pillow, never wanting to see the light of day again.

The next morning, as I set about my morning routine with Colin, reading books in our reading room amidst the stuffed animals, he pointed to my lip and said, "Mama heal ouch." I hugged him and felt empty.

When Dylan woke up an hour later he called down to me loudly, "What happened, Mama? Everything is *totally* different! What is going on?"

He came into the reading room and looked at my lip.

He was silent.

"He's gone, isn't he?" Dylan whispered.

I nodded.

He said, "Good."

The boys ate breakfast, but the cut on my lip was too raw to eat anything without stinging. Since the cupboards were bare, I had to do groceries, but in my humiliation I drove to a grocery store twenty minutes outside of Boulder rather than face my townspeople with a bruised lip. Two women in the store gave me an extra look and then a sad smile, and I felt shamed, humiliated and alone. But lips heal quickly, and I was scabbed over the next day, though forever different.

As I mashed hard-boiled eggs for a sandwich, my cell phone kept ringing. I noticed my mother-in-law's area code, but didn't answer it, until her persistence required attention. I answered and without greeting asked her what she wanted.

"Corinne!" she yelled and I moved the phone away from my ear. "What is going on? Ted just left a message from JAIL!" She was hysterical.

I told her about the fight and Ted's behavior. She didn't ask if I was okay, nor did she ask about my children. "He has to work," she said. "His boss will worry about him!"

Her husband got on the phone and told me that Ted should have been released already, but nothing could be done, meaning he had to stay another night because of the holiday, and why did I call the police for some silly argument?

I was sleep-deprived and in shock, so I had no idea what she was talking about. "Holiday?"

"Columbus Day," Gerard said. "My God, what is wrong with you?"

I snapped. "Well, you see, Gerard, *your* son, *my husband*, has an abusive temper, is in jail, and I am, well, how can you say, absolutely heartbroken and upset?"

"Tell someone who cares," Gerard said, "We have to talk about getting Ted out of jail."

"I don't have to talk to you," I said, and I hung up.

He called back. "Corinne, this is Gerard again. It is a holiday. You need to call the office and tell them Ted has the flu and won't be in today."

"Oh," I said, "that's right, they work today. Forgot about the holiday."

He yelled, "You should have thought about that before calling the police, you dummy."

I yelled back, "*Your asshole son* should have thought of that before splitting my lip you old man, and by the way, thanks for asking, but I am doing fine and the boys are okay too. I see where Ted gets it all, Gerard. Don't think I don't know exactly where he gets this from: you and your scornful, no-one-is- good-enough-for wife!"

"Why you...." he began, but I hung up. Then I left a message at Ted's employer. saying he was sick, and continued making the boys lunch.

Two days later, the boys and I were riding our bikes along the creek trail when Ted was released from jail. His parents' lawyer had begun a process to reduce the charge to harassment and had been calling me to talk about modifying the restraining order so Ted to could return home. I refused, but agreed to his suggestion that I request he be able to see me and the boys in public places.

Walking through the security gate of the courthouse with Colin in his expensive stroller, Dylan in his GAP clothes and my almost $7,000 diamond ring on my finger, I had to go to the DA's office to request a modification of the restraining order. "Your husband the new guy working here?" the guy had asked as I handed him my pocketbook. To my tearful expression he said, "Guess not."

A receptionist behind a glass window, chewing gum, instructed me to sit down and wait for the forms necessary to modify a restraining order. I felt humiliated, shamed and embarrassed, as if I was in someone else's life.

"Cute kids!" the receptionist smiled at me.

I felt nauseous, and quickly remembered where the bathroom had been along the hall.

To distract myself, I opened my pocketbook and found a pamphlet given to me by a victim's advocate with big bold letters asking *Why does she stay?* Opening it up were paragraphs with explanations under subtitles like *low self-esteem, financial concerns* and *thinks she should be treated this way* and *for the chidren* and *denial.*

"Absolute morons!" I said, out loud by mistake.

The receptionist looked at me, the pamphlet, cracked her gum and smiled knowingly. Something unspoken passed between us.

Only three years ago I had entertained these exact hypothetical conversations myself in casual social settings, curious about the same phenomenon: why on earth did a woman stay in an abusive marriage? I sat there holding back my stinging tears, remembering the cushion of cozy distance the 'she' used to have in my mind thinking of abused women as "the other." I sat in pain, embarrassment and utter desolation; waiting for paperwork to modify my husband's restraining order.

I took a huge breath. Both of my sons looked up at me, and I managed a smile. I closed the pamphlet and put it back in my pocketbook, wanting to scream out in a frantic cry,

The woman is trying to leave! She is learning to have her voice heard and respected. She is growing out of crazy, and her husband is scared and cannot imagine life with a healthy wife. His entire existence is about putting her down so he can feel normal, and she is desperately clinging to any strength of self, wanting to save her children from the hatred, and anger, only to have her only support, the man who was supposed to partner with her, turn on her in hostility and manipulations. Don't they know this entire relationship is about leaving? From the start, a trap, guilt for not loving a man who offers such adoration, a man who claims undying affection—initially she feels like shit for wanting to leave, is told she has problems for wanting to leave, decides she must leave and faces the wrath from a man everyone sees as perfect. She is a woman in transition, going from a wounded, angry, hostile and reactive girl in a grown body to a woman who believes in healthy living, doesn't want to take anger out on others anymore, and wants to protect her children. She is learning to listen to her instinct, think for herself and respect her life. These are women in transition, damn it, not victims of abuse, in the process of making a new life. We are punished by the part-

ners we chose who hide their dysfunction behind us, and when we stop playing they go crazy on us, and we want to leave—the whole relationship is about leaving, and finding that strength of self!

I sighed, and looked at my sons—children of domestic violence—and let the tears stream down my face. The gum-chewing receptionist brought me a box of tissues and rested her hand on my shoulder. "It'll be okay honey, it hurts at first, but now, you know, you gotta get out of it all. Only you can do this, and you gotta do it for them." She waved a finger at my boys for emphasis before returning to her desk.

Letting my thoughts wander, I remembered the night of my husband's arrest. The female officer had said in sympathy, "I was married to an asshole too, no kids, thank God, but I got out, you can too, it gets better, you have to get the strength."

I had shuddered, not wanting to be a part of the never-ending gender war that I was supposed to rally around. I had been tempted to say "This is all a mistake" or to explain, "I used to intern in an office similar to this one in southern California" or "My husband isn't so bad, just upset that I want to divorce" and "He loves me still" and "He's afraid to be alone."

Looking around the waiting room, my eyes rested on the receptionist answering her phone calls. As I gazed, paused and cleared my thoughts, I saw who she saw me to be: a victim of domestic violence. And no matter how many times I blinked or swallowed the lump in my throat, or tried to launch myself into another reality, this woman saw me as "one of those women" and seeing myself as she saw me was the bravest and hardest thing I could do. And although the opportunity had presented itself before—with the man in the parking lot by my husband's office, or the look on my neighbors' faces—it wasn't until I saw this woman look at me, a woman who likely made less money in four years than my husband made in one, that I finally listened and just stayed still, letting myself see how I was seen by others.

Once the amendments were made to the restraining order, we met with Ted in playgrounds, but he was distracted and full of self-pity and self-involvement, calling anyone he knew, people he hadn't spoken to in decades, to complain about me. All I could do was watch him enjoy playing the bigger-victim game.

My parents visited to help with the hand-offs, as Ted and I were not supposed to talk, even to exchange the boys. Ted was surprisingly respectful of the police presence in our life. During her visit my mother offered up that I was clearly manic-depressive and selfish to not take medication for my illness, although she hadn't seen me since our luncheon when Dylan was a baby. She also felt that

"Poor Ted didn't have to go through all of this," and "Clearly I was making a lot about nothing," to the point of calling me a "femme fatale." "You don't even have a scar on your lip," she told me. "Did you really need to do this to him? You can be quite provocative, you know." Finally I abruptly dismissed her, refusing any more of her so-called help. In the months that followed, she sent me books on various mental illnesses, telling me that divorcing Ted was wrong, and that it was high time I got help for my mental problem. She even called psychologists in Boulder to make appointments for me. She also made sure to have me know that if Ted decided to take this to court, she'd testify against me. In contrast, Ted's family welcomed him with open arms. As the victim of such an out-of-control woman, he was to be coddled and soothed for his ordeal in jail.

My sleeping, however, had vastly improved now that the house was mine. Ted was too scared to bother me there for fear of the police.

One day I overheard him talking to a friend on his cell phone. "Yeah," he said with a laugh, "got caught doing stuff I shouldn't have been doing.... . she played a good move."

I ran up to him, the pain in my heart overwhelming. "You knew all along?"

He hung up on his friend and stared at me with a mild smirk.

"You knew? You knew? You knew!" I repeated and whispered until I fell in a heap of tears on the grass.

That night my breast milk dried up. Colin cried himself to sleep during what should have been his 3 a.m. feed. I held him to my empty breast, feeling like a terrible mother.

In December, Ted's company laid off thirty percent of their staff, and Ted was jobless but still bought me a brand new ski parka from LLBean in chocolate brown for Christmas. Opening the gift, I stared at it, my mouth gaping open for minutes, knowing he never knew what I wanted, he couldn't ever give me the love I wanted. Whenever I wore that coat, I felt cold despite the puffy down feathers and fluffy hood. Throughout the holiday season and beyond, he interviewed quite a lot, and by the end of January, he had, on the Friday of Super Bowl weekend—the ten-year anniversary of the night we met on that cold and drizzly Friday night at a sports bar in San Jose—three offers: one for a job in Minnesota, another in California and another in Massachusetts, at a big company that offered a complete relocation package, no maximum, including taking care of our lease and an attractive salary—over six figures.

When the offer came in, Dylan was at a program for home-schooled kids that I'd found a week earlier, and Colin was taking a nap in his car seat as Ted and I had negotiated an additional 15K on his offer.

"I'm not going," I said as he closed his cell phone, having received the final verbal offer.

Pausing to think, he flipped his phone cover up and down, while scratching his head.

"It's our chance, Corinne, we can go back now," he said sheepishly. "It'll all be covered," he said. "They'll move all our shit, and our stock will IPO soon. We can get a great house and go back to that life … Corinne?"

"No, Ted, our chance is done." I cried unabashedly, pulling the car to the nearest exit to park in a Target parking lot.

He stared at the floor, eyes unmoving while I sobbed. He offered me his sleeve to wipe my tears on, and I cried even harder.

"You know, the Boulderites will never let you fit in, a woman like you." He paused and looked me out of the corner of his eye.

"Huh?" I continued sobbing.

"After what I did," he explained—"small town, gossipy—you'll never make friends here. They'll all know."

To my questioning expression, he shrugged his shoulders. "Do I have to explain everything to you?" Then he stated more softly, "Boulderites. I know how they are; they'll never accept a woman coming from the marriage we had. Might pretend to, or be polite about it, but a real friend, no way. They'll keep you at arm's length, and you'll be on the outside looking in all the time. You'll never be accepted in Boulder, Corinne, never."

It finally clicked for me. "Oh, the domestic violence!"

He flinched, and then said, "Yes."

I thought for awhile.

"You'll be lonely here," he said. "You'll have no friends."

After wiping my eyes with the back of my hand, I whispered, "I don't care, Ted, I just don't care, this about *the boys and their life*, and if I don't have a friend living here, I just don't care because I have to look in those boys' eyes, and when I am a white-haired little old lady, being their mother is what will matter most." My tears rolled down my cheeks the entire drive home.

In fact I sobbed from one o'clock on Friday when the job offer came until Sunday evening when the Super Bowl was on. I took only brief periods that weekend to drink water, eat a few bites of bread and to sleep in fifteen-minute intervals. I cried so hard I could barely open my eyes, and Ted took care of the boys all by himself.

We were done. And we both knew it.

Ten years, two kids, lots of pain and finally, freedom.

Ted had lined his suitcases along the Departures sidewalk of Denver International Airport; I was wearing the same sweats I'd worn for three days, my hair in a greasy ponytail.

"Have a good flight!" I waved through the passenger window, my voice crackling with emotion.

Ted hugged both boys in the backseat and then offered me open arms too. But I shook my head, tears streaming down my face. "No, it would be too hard," I said, "I am sorry. I'd never be able to let go!"

He nodded.

I called his name and he put his head into the window. "This was never about hurting you," I said. "Wanting to divorce, I mean. It was always, from the start, from as far back as living in Massachusetts, this was one hundred percent all about saving the boys from *us*. I wanted to save them from our stuff, Ted, and you couldn't do it with me. I'll be sad forever for that." I began to sob, then took a deep breath. "I'll be sad for that for the rest of my life. I'll wish you could have grown up with me and faced this stuff, and I will never be able to tell you how excruciatingly painful it is to choose between your children and your husband—a choice *no* woman should ever have to make. I know you understand this somewhere deep inside. I know you know, you know. Oh, Ted, this has never been about love; it's been about saving the boys from it all, breaking the cycle. You know this, right?"

Crying overcame me.

He reached in, touched my arm, looked me right into my eyes and whispered, "I do, Corinne, I do understand...."

I hung my head and cried big sobs as he stepped through the moving doors, turning back to look at us only once with the face of a man who'd lost everything that ever meant anything to him.

I felt a pain in my chest as if my heart were ripping into two pieces, right down the middle. My healing was coming at the cost of a dear loved one, watching my husband get sicker and sicker as I began to grow beyond the living wounded. There was nothing I could do except watch him leave—despite my impulse to change my mind, move to Massachusetts, say it was all going to be all right and run after him with the kids. Instead I sat still and let the pain rip my heart in two pieces right there at the Denver Airport departure lot.

Driving back to Boulder in the evening dusk, with Raffi singing songs to my sons, I realized that aside from my therapist and my hairdresser, I knew no one in Boulder—no neighbors, no friends, no one. I was totally and completely alone, with two boys relying on me to make it all better for them.

That night, after the boys were in bed, I cried for half the night before I fell asleep, with no choice but to wake up in Boulder, all by myself, to take care of my sons—alone, terrified, pained and wondering if there had been anything I could have done differently to save my marriage.

978-0-595-49053-0
0-595-49053-0